# APPRENTICED TO HOPE

# APPRENTICED TO HOPE

## A SOURCEBOOK FOR DIFFICULT TIMES

Julie Neraas

Augsburg Books

MINNEAPOLIS

APPRENTICED TO HOPE
A Sourcebook for Difficult Times
Living Well Series

Cover art: © Digital Vision Ltd./SuperStock
Cover design: Christy J. P. Barker
Interior design: Michelle L. N. Cook

Library of Congress Cataloging-in-Publication Data
Neraas, Julie, 1954-
  Apprenticed to hope : a sourcebook for difficult times / Julie Neraas.
     p. cm. — (Living well series)
  Includes bibliographical references.
  ISBN 978-0-8066-5764-6 (alk. paper)
  1. Hope—Religious aspects—Christianity. I. Title.
  BV4638.N47 2009
  234'.25—dc22        2008043279

# CONTENTS

*Acknowledgments*                                       vii

*Prologue: Being Apprenticed to Hope*                    ix

## Part One: The Nature of Hope
1. The Nature of Hope                                      2
2. Hope Differs from Optimism                             5
3. Living with a Beast                                    8
4. Hope's Limits                                         14
5. Hope and Imagination                                  17
6. Help—Hope's Companion                                 23
7. Our Heritage of Hope                                  27
8. The Anchor—Symbol of Hope                             34
9. Borrowing Hope                                        37
10. Hope as a Choice                                     41
11. Mature Hope                                          45

## Part Two: Threats to Hope
12. Relapse and Its Emotional Fallout                    50
13. Other Threats to Hope                                54
14. Spiritual Fallout: Illness "Can Ruin Your Manners
    toward God"                       58
15. False Hope                                           63
16. Provisional Hope                                     66

**Part Three: Hope's Siblings: Truth, Faith, Meaning**

17. Finding Meaning Trumps Particular Outcomes          70
18. Hope Seeks the Bigger Picture                       72
19. Hope's Relationship to Faith                        80
20. Hope and Truth Sit Side by Side                     86
21. When Hope Takes Work                                90

**Part Four: Aids to Hope—Sources of Hope**

22. Detecting Patterns—A Cause for Hope                 94
23. How Hope Returns                                    98
24. Sheltering Hope                                     106
25. Stories Can Be Medicine                             108
26. In Praise of Coping                                 112
27. Surprising Sources of Hope                          120
28. Humanistic Hope                                     122
29. Hope and History                                    129
30. Hope and God                                        132
31. Hope as Partnership between Human and Divine        136
32. Hope's Origins in Mystery                           141

*A Concluding Personal Word*                            144
*Questions for Reflection and Discussion*               145
*Notes*                                                 155

# ACKNOWLEDGMENTS

A problem for some of us who are extroverted by nature—at least the problem for me—is that I do not think very well alone. I need to talk out loud with another person in order to get clear about what I think. This can hamper the writing process because it is not always possible to gather a circle for coffee and conversation in the middle of the day. Consequently, I inserted myself, for several years, right into the middle of many a dinner party, many a walk around one of our Minnesota lakes, and many a car ride, asking people to think aloud with me. "Could you spare fifteen minutes on false hope?" I would ask. Or "Talk to me about what role the Depression played in your parents' and grandparents' worldview." For this I want to thank many dear friends, family members, and mentors: Patricia Bachmeier, Carol Dunsmore, Heidi Bryan, Elizabeth Toohey, Deborah Dewey, Ted Loder, Liz Dooley, Nancy Schongalla-Bowman, Betty Grant, Kate Brady, Kate Sandweiss, Gerald Richman, Kathy Coskran, Gail Goeller, Barbara Arnery, Kitty Leighton, Jan Bucher, Amy Barber, Kathryn, Nancy, Bev and Don Neraas, and Harry Cartales.

I owe special thanks to Margaret Todd Maitland, friend and writer extraordinare, whose literary coattails I hung on to gladly on many a Friday afternoon at the Minneapolis Institute of Art, where we read to each other our latest writing. I am also grateful to Susan Deborah (Sam) King and to Gail Goeller, who generously read through midpoint drafts, lending their keen writers' eyes.

To my generous colleagues at Hamline University, who willingly read early drafts, often at times that were inconvenient for them. For their encouragement and skill at editing, I want to thank Scott Edelstein, Pat Francisco, and Deborah Keenan. I also want to express my appreciation for the gentle but persistent urging of my colleague and boss, Mary Rockcastle, to get writing. Thanks also to Joan Mitchell, CSJ, for her publishing savvy, to Gail Milstein, for permission to use her interview of Patty Wetterling, and to Scott Edelstein and Patricia Kirkpatrick for their help with this title.

My greatest hope for this book is that it will get you interested in your own heritage of hope, and that you might come to appreciate hope's power.

—Julie Neraas

# PROLOGUE:
# BEING APPRENTICED TO HOPE

I have been apprenticed to hope for a long time now; my learning laboratories and teachers have been many. As for any child, my early learning took place in my family, where I absorbed the outlook and worldview of my parents and grandparents as unconsciously as drawing in breath. In later years, I was a more conscious apprentice, especially while working in settings where hope is tested, as a chaplain—in a miserable prison in inner-city Philadelphia, in a treatment center for people with drug and alcohol addiction, and on three college campuses—and as a minister in several churches.

My most demanding teacher by far has been a chronic illness, which has kept me tethered, for nearly ten years, to the gritty, day-to-day (sometimes hour-to-hour), back-to-the-wall, unglamorous work of coping and the inevitable cycles of losing hope and finding it again. Illness grabbed me by the neck, thrust me into the fire, and swung me around with dizzying force, year after year, dissolving old assumptions, rupturing old identities, exposing easy answers, and complicating my relationship with hope.

In my mind's eye, I see myself in my early twenties, teaching tennis in the blazing summer heat, hopping from one city park to another from dawn till dusk in my little orange Fiat, its backseat stuffed to the gills with tennis balls, coming home in the late evening with energy to spare. In the next frame I see myself lying on the sofa on another summer day, twenty (or more years) later, marooned and near despair over the fifth summer in a row that I had been knocked flat by another devastating relapse. I could not have walked even a few blocks on such a day.

This ongoing bout with illness has left me alternately subdued, bewildered, furious, sad, distraught, resigned, angry, combative, and grateful. Yet this trial has also strengthened my relationship with hope, making my reaching for it all the more conscious. While chronic illness has been my most difficult challenge, I believe each of us has a beast of one kind or another living in our house. What is yours?

Just as *you*, my reader, have had to face whatever challenges life has delivered up, navigating the currents in various life arenas—health and work, family and friendship, citizenship in a community, country, and global family—*you also* have a relationship with hope, and it is my aim to get you interested in that relationship and help you become even more conscious of it. What is it that has most challenged your hope? What has most strengthened it? And how do you nourish hope when it needs nourishing?

Looking back on it now, I see that my apprenticeship to hope began unconsciously when I was a teenager, living through the inevitable emotional turbulence of that age in a family that favored the upbeat and positive. In retrospect, I wonder if cheer was shored up as it was because my parents wanted to protect me and my siblings from an emotion we did not know quite how to deal with— call it melancholy, call it gloom, call it depression, traits sometimes associated with Scandinavians. While I was not conscious of this at the time, I needed to stake out a middle ground between these extremes. Hope is just such a middle ground.

In this long season of illness, I have been surprised to discover that a fierceness resides in me that exhibits all the busyness and fury of a small, persistent animal. It digs and digs, bites and claws at any corral that threatens to fence it in. Maybe this is hope with an attitude. At times I have wondered whether it is just plain denial and delusion, as we used to say of those in treatment who could not face the truth squarely. I no longer think so. It is unyielding, unrelenting hope, renegade hope jumping fences I thought would have restrained her. But no, there she is, having leapt over yet another barrier in her effort to shake free of the despair that grabs at hope's heels.

At its best this is how hope works: it holds stubbornly to a better future, without a precise timetable or illusions about specific outcomes. Hope is a clear-eyed risk taker. Bless you, stubborn hope.

Illness has taught me that as the body goes, so goes hope. Try as we might to spiritualize it, hope's rising and waning is often (though not always) tied to our physical well-being. Feeling healthy and rested makes a big difference in the vitality of our hope.

In her famous poem likening hope to "the thing with feathers—that perches in the soul," Emily Dickinson says of hope: "Yet never in Extremity / It asked a crumb—of me."[1] Is she suggesting that in extreme circumstances, when we lack even the energy to reach for hope, it may come as a free gift, without effort? If this is her meaning, I heartily agree. Sometimes hope *does* come as an outright gift. But my experience is that it does not always come free. Quite to the contrary, hope can be exacting and ferocious in its demands. In some seasons, just to stay within its range requires sheer tenacity and perseverance.

To birth hope in such times—even to assume a hopeful posture—is a great achievement. When all the paths you have tried lead to dead ends, and you see nothing but closed doors, the energy of hope is the hatchet with which you break down doors. This brand of hope is muscular; it actively scans the horizon for options, hypothesizes solutions, and considers possible ways forward.

We would not want to live on hope alone. Hope is not an end in itself, or simply a stopgap that enables us to remain idling in the present. Hope is a bridge from the present to the future. It is forward leaning. And eventually it must deliver; it must give birth to something. Otherwise it sours, dissolving into discouragement, anger, resentment, even depression. In the thick of illness I did not want more hope; I wanted health. People who are poor don't want more hope; they want its tangible manifestations: enough food, adequate clothing, a place to call home, a decent job, dignity, and choices. Those ravaged by war do not want to cling to hope forever; they want to live in peace. It is not enough to go on hoping for a future that has no intimations in the present.

While despair has not claimed a regular place at my table, I have had to wrestle with it for sure. I have been most vulnerable to despair when I have worked for weeks to climb—millimeter by millimeter—out of the deep hole of a relapse, only to be yanked back down the hill again. Symptoms, which had been temporarily more muted, yelled and screamed to beat the band, with my body in all-out rebellion. If hope is energized and sustained by confidence that one is getting somewhere, I have had long seasons of getting nowhere, or worse, regressing quickly, flung down, time and again, like Sisyphus and that detestable rock that kept rolling back down the hill. It is this sense of entrapment, of no way out, that characterizes despair. This illness has seemed endless to me. Its emotional and spiritual fallout is a subject I will return to in chapters to come.

## A Caveat

Despite this health crisis, I am a privileged person, both materially and emotionally. I have never had to struggle for life's basic necessities—far from it. Many of my day-to-day expectations, like freedom from harm, abundant food, more than adequate shelter, meaningful work, faithful friends, a loyal family, health care, and citizenship in a democracy are expectations the majority of earth's people cannot even imagine, let alone realize. Still, I want a mature hope that does more than simply float on a sea of privilege, rising and falling with particular outcomes in my personal life, including the blessing of health. Illness has forced me to broaden hope's terms and come to know it in a wider field.

Having had my own share of ups and downs, and having spent many years considering this subject, I thought my understanding of hope was rooted in the muck of real life, not in the ether of rational thought. But in the unmasking caused by long illness, I realized that it's a very different thing to labor toward hope in the midst of a physical trial that saps every reserve of energy, patience, and fortitude, leaving you raw and diminished.

Even in the throes of illness I have had access to resources. By that I mean medical care and the help of friends and family who brought me food, drove me to doctor's appointments, taught my classes, and helped me with household chores. While these privileges did not blunt physical pain, they certainly helped me deal with the difficulties of illness. I never felt completely alone, and cannot imagine how people cope when they *are* alone.

## WHY HOPE IS INTRIGUING

One of the occupational hazards in my line of work is that I get to hear about people's terrible experiences with religion whether I want to or not. The ruthless nun, the dogmatic tradition, the rigid family, the sexual indiscretions of a priest, minister, rabbi, or meditation teacher. When many hear that I am an ordained clergywoman, they grab for that tired, if perennially appropriate, label "hypocrite" when referring to religious people. Having been in a long-term "lovers' quarrel" (a term coined by Rev. William Sloane Coffin) with my own religious tradition, I am sometimes saddened and often sickened by the ways religion can be used as a wedge and a weapon, drawing lines and erecting barriers that exclude people in the name of purity. Religion is supposed to be about that which binds us to each other in our mutual dependence upon God and one another. (The Latin *religio* means "to bind together." Or, in Arabic, as Islam would have it, the closest word to "religion" is *din*, or *al-day*, which means to pay one's debts to God.) Sometimes I feel like screaming at those who use religion divisively: "All right, all of you, come out of your sanctuaries with your hands up! And by the way, leave your holy books behind!"

Hope, in contrast with religion, seems refreshingly spacious. It is roomier and more inclusive because it does not require assent to particular beliefs, nor is it wedded to ideology. Indeed, hope, while necessary to our well-being, can exist with equal strength *within* religious traditions and *outside* of them.

Hope is compelling because it is universal. It crosses all human boundaries: age, race, class, gender, ethnicity, and religious, political, or any other persuasion. Everyone needs it, and almost everyone exhibits at least some measure of hope if they have made it as far as this day. For where there is hope, there is life. And where there is no hope, life is greatly diminished. In fact, to live without hope is to barely live at all. The capacity to hope is an indispensable human quality; even in times of crisis when confidence and trust have been broken, hope sustains us in our living.

# IRONIES

Given its primacy and its power, there are a number of ironies surrounding hope. First among them is why we pay so little attention to hope until we feel it ebbing away or are in desperate need of recovering it. We cannot live without hope, after all. In fact, when people are deeply depressed and sorely lacking in hope, we send them to the hospital, or at the very least, to a doctor. Furthermore, we seem to know less about hope than we do about faith and love, with which hope is often bound in as a theological triplet.

We often speak of hope casually, off-handedly: "I hope the sun will come out today," we say, or, to fill a gap in the conversation: "I hope you have a good trip." In other situations, hope is treated like a trifling consolation. I was playing tennis not long ago when I heard a man on an adjacent court say to his doubles partner, "Gee, Fred, I thought you had nothing more than a hope and a prayer on that shot," as if hope and prayer were trivial and of little consequence. I know of nothing more fundamental or powerful than hope or prayer, with the exception of love. Sometimes when we speak of hope, we really mean something closer to despair. I asked my brother-in-law, Harry, recently if he thought he would be able to play basketball after his hip surgery. "Well, one can always hope," he said, meaning, quite probably, "No."

One of the stereotypes I want to debunk is that hope is nothing much, a mere feeling, like a dollop of cream atop the soup perhaps, but insubstantial in itself. An unfortunate result of Emily Dickinson's oft-quoted reference to hope as "the thing with feathers" is that it can leave a person asking, what does something so ethereal have to commend it to a world full of beasts with fangs? To put it bluntly, as Rev. James Gertmenian of Plymouth Congregational Church in Minneapolis asked: "Is hope an undersized David staring up at the Goliath of Earth's troubles, with nothing more than a slingshot as a tool?" Would you bet money on hope? I would, and I aim to show you why.

# HOPE IS ESSENTIAL

There is a deep human intuition of hope. Like an invisible signature in the life of a person or community, hope may say more about the soul of a person, or the outlook of a group, than about the material circumstances of that individual or community's life.

Fannie Lou Hamer was the youngest of twenty children in a sharecropper's family from Mississippi. So poor that she and her siblings often went hungry, their mother tied her children's feet in sacks when they worked in the fields because they did not have enough money for shoes. Having lived under the heel of white people all her life, she earned less than four dollars a day in the cotton fields; yet when civil rights workers arrived, talking about the power of the vote, she began to realize that by voting, she and others who had been persecuted by white officials had the power to vote them out of office. When civil rights workers asked for volunteers to register others, she raised her hand, aware of the certainty of white reprisal. The flicker of hope for change overrode all her fears. After all, "The only thing they could do to me was kill me," she said, "and it seemed like they'd been trying to do that . . . ever since I could remember."[2]

In order to act on her hope, Hamer had to be willing to move past fear and defy the odds. By embodying the hope she sought for others as well as for herself, she brought more hope into being. Hopefulness is not a commodity we find; it is something we become. For Hamer, the price for moving toward the right to vote was a willingness to be punished by the white establishment for doing so. Hope required stoutheartedness.

Sometimes hope's presence is visible and palpable; it rises to the surface and you see it shining in a person's spirit, or in the attitude and actions of a group. At other times, hope hums silently beneath the surface, content to do its work in the background. It lives at a layer of reality far deeper and far less visible than anything that might call forth hopefulness. It is the essential core of human life, beyond reason. Beyond expectation. Beyond what might be dreamed.

Hope may be our greatest need in this dark time, its viability our greatest question. In a world of unrelenting violence and war, riddled with savage inequalities, unfathomable injustices, armies of greed, phalanxes of corruption, all manner of addictions, threats to the environment, the loss of another species every twenty minutes, looming water shortages, and a burgeoning population beyond what a withering planet can sustain, the threats to hope are legion. The headlines of most any newspaper are more than enough to drive any of us to collapse in despair.

It has been estimated that of roughly 3,500 years of recorded history, somewhere near 3,144 have been years of war. In the last century alone, one hundred million people died in wars, the majority of them civilians. With this as our lineage, we are right to ask whether hope and history ever truly meet. With this as our lineage, hope has an outrageous component to it. We need not even mention words like Auschwitz, Sarajevo, or Rwanda to underscore what terrible things we human beings inflict on one another. Belief in human progress can seem suspect; hope a risk, veiled in mourning. Shall we then counsel despair? Of course not. What can we bring to the world if not hope?

Political movements come and go, and while the litany of wars and other, lesser conflicts continues unabated, this is only one way to read history. Beneath the media's radar and the dramatic, deadly, or threatening events that garner the most attention, countless quiet acts of goodness unfold day after day, year after year. In any given community on any given day, most children are fed, clothed, nurtured, and educated. Elderly people and other vulnerable folk are cared for with kindness and respect. Someone, somewhere is standing up for justice. Somewhere, someone is going the extra mile for another. Somewhere, earth's bounty and beauty are made manifest, right this very minute.

Whether you say of yourself that you are, by and large, a hopeful person, or one who lives most days without hope, "it's a fair enough vocation to strike one match after another against the dark isolation, when spectacular arrogance rules the day and tries to force hope into hiding."[3] Given the many threats to hope, we need to fortify it and bring hope out into the open.

One of the remarkable characteristics of hope is this: as with the miniscule mustard seed, size has absolutely no relation to strength. Just a tiny amount of the right ingredient is potent. A small measure of leaven is enough to raise the whole loaf; a pinch of salt can radically alter the taste of a dish. The homeopathic remedy I take consists of tiny pellets of condensed fennel, and I mean tiny: the size of a pinhead. They are so small I have to put on my glasses when I count out a dose, yet they have been far and away the most effective treatment in a decade of trials and errors with countless other medicines and potential cures.

Even a flicker of hope can make all the difference for a person or community. Hope grows and flourishes when there is even the slightest evidence of progress. An acquaintance of mine works on behalf of refugees around the world. She has just returned from two weeks in Sierra Leone, a country of unfathomable poverty and political unrest. Sanitation is terrible there, hunger is rampant, roofless hut homes in outlying areas offer no protection from torrential rains. Yet she said of the people she met: They have a very small bit of hope, but they make it last a long time and stretch it a long ways. They embody hope as "a dimension of the spirit, an orientation of the heart."[4]

## SPEAKING IN TWO VOICES

In the chapters to follow I will work in two voices. The first is a reflective voice that comes from being a lifelong student of literature, theology, psychology, and poetry. As a teacher who continues to teach a graduate course entitled "The Heritage of Hope," I am forever combing bookstores in search of what our most astute thinkers and writers have to say about this subject. The second voice, which I think of as my coauthor, is that of my body, a rather raw and uncensored voice that illness has taught me to respect. By doing so, I am heeding the advice of poet Charles Olson, who offers this counsel:

Whatever you have to say, leave
the roots on, let them
dangle

And the dirt

Just to make clear
where they came from.[5]

I *will* leave the roots on, laying bare the truths and discoveries I have come
to through my body, including face-to-face meetings with my limitations and
vulnerabilities, as well as a palpable resurgence of health and hope. My bodily
self will no longer allow my mind to run roughshod over her, as if I had no obli-
gation to my physical being. In concert together, these two voices bring a wider
perspective on hope than either of them could alone.

Like my Swedish grandmothers, whose holiday tables were laden with a
broad array of dishes (called smorgasbords), you can take a plate and dish yourself up here, beginning with any chapter that draws you in. Each chapter can be
read alone. You will encounter perspectives on hope from a variety of sources, as
well as different ways to think about hope. In chapters to come, I reflect on hope's
gifted quality, its relationship to the imagination and our need for meaning, as
well as the way it's bound up with help and community. I consider different kinds
and levels of hope, distinguish it from optimism and from faith, compare false
hope with the real thing, and paint a portrait of mature hope. If this material has
done its job, it will have engaged you in uncovering your own heritage of hope
and in recognizing its patterns and powers in your life.

# PART ONE
# THE NATURE OF HOPE

# 1.

# THE NATURE OF HOPE

*The very least you can do in your life is to figure out what to hope for. And the most you can do is live inside that hope. Not admire it from a distance but live right in it, under its roof.*[6]

With hope, so much is possible. Without it, so little is. Many people live without explicitly religious faith. Others live without much, if any, love. But people do not survive long without hope. Hope is a powerful conduit between our individual, local lives and the Great Mystery infusing and upholding us. It's a place where energy gathers. Sometimes, hope is visible; you can see it in the light in people's eyes and in the energy of a community. At other times, it remains hidden, stirring in a would-be immigrant the desire to go in search of a better shore.

At its core, hope is the sense of a way forward, of possibility, even in trouble or despair. It is a feeling that things can work out, that we will somehow find the necessary resources to handle whatever life delivers up. It is a sense that we will find the necessary resources to meet our needs. Hope must surely be "the basest instinct," writes Barbara Kingsolver, "baser even than hate. If the world of living has to turn on the single point of remaining alive, that pointed endurance is the poetry of hope."[7]

Hope is the experience of enlargement; it looks through the present to a wider field from which to draw the resources to move forward. When it seems like there is nothing but dead ends and no-exits, hope is the capacity to keep looking; it is "an axe you break the down doors with in an emergency."[8]

We often take hope for granted, like a private, interior resource that we tend and nourish when times are good, trusting it will be there for us when times are tough. If hope has been there in the past, we assume it will be there in the future. However, it is when our hope is threatened and it feels like there are no internal resources to draw on that we consciously reach for it. At such times we wonder: Can hope be nurtured? How might a person get in position to receive hope?

It may not be possible to know what it's like to live without hope until you yourself have entered into despair and had a taste of hope's absence. I mean the experience of being down on your luck, down on your knees, face on the ground, with dirt in your mouth. "No understanding of hope can be honest unless it reckons with the absence of hope, the dark night of the soul when nothing comforts and nothing reassures."[9] This kind of experience can reveal hope's power.

Trying times notwithstanding, hope is not just for times of crisis. It is present moment to moment as we look to the future. Hope sends a farmer into the fields, a student to school, an athlete to practice, an addict to AA. Hope is a mother putting on boxing gloves on behalf of her child's battle with serious illness. It can be *that* fierce a commitment, a holding fast to a desired outcome, and it can be *that* nimble regarding *what* the outcome might be. Hope is an energy that chooses life regardless of present circumstances. Hope is the return we want most from any visit to a doctor. Hope is the fisherman plumbing the sea with the thinnest of lines. It undergirds the decision to birth a child. Hope is the medical researcher experimenting, through trial and error, toward a treatment for cancer. Hope can be a quiet companion or an explosive force, propelling an individual or community to action.

Some people have to struggle hard for their hope. Others seem to have it so easily; they wake up in the morning and it's simply there, dependably, a learned confidence in life. When you are hopeful, you trust that even when life delivers hard challenges you will find a way to meet them.

Given what we now know about how utterly determinative are chemical balances/imbalances, hormone levels, genetic makeup, and the environment on a person's health and well-being, maybe we are growing more compassionate toward those who must struggle toward hope through the jungle of depression or mental illness. We know that trying harder counts for little, if anything, when one's biochemistry is "off."

Like the air we breathe, hope cannot be bought or sold, hoarded or stolen. It cannot be possessed or made permanent; it must be renewed again and again. The good news is that hope is a constantly renewable resource, and, happily, it can be shared, nurtured—even borrowed, if necessary.

Hope has healing properties. A compassionate physician speaks of a patient's right to hope and gives it the highest possible praise. "True hope has proved as important as any medication I might prescribe or any procedure I might perform," writes Dr. Jerome Groopman.[10] While hope is a strengthening force, it also lays a person open to the vulnerabilities of love, desire, expectation, disappointment, loss. "Maybe I shouldn't get my hopes up," we counsel ourselves, tempering our expectations and armoring ourselves with reason, aware that to acknowledge a particular hope may expose a deep desire or heartfelt yearning that we need to protect. "To hope is to gamble . . . to bet on the future, and on your desires. Yet it is the opposite of fear, for to live is to risk."[11]

One of hope's central characteristics is its ability to adapt. The content or object of hope can shift without hope itself being lost. Consider this example: You have a friend going in for medical tests, and you hope mightily, for as long as possible, that this does not spell cancer. If the diagnosis turns out to be cancer, hope shifts. Its focus now is on effective treatments. You lean hard into that hope, yet stay open to all possible sources of healing. If a remission or cure becomes impossible, you hope that the living of this life can be as full as possible, that the ill person's dignity will be honored and his pain manageable. After that, you hope that when death arrives, it comes gently.

In their desire to find narratives that personify hope, thoughtful people down through the centuries have drawn on the myth of Pandora, of Greek legend. Recall that she was endowed by the gods with all good graces. Her father, Zeus, had given her to Epimetheus, who was immediately smitten by her beauty and, dispensing with courtship altogether (a custom of the gods), simply made her his wife. Her new husband gave to Pandora the gift of a large earthenware jar, with one caveat; ah yes, that inevitable—and lethal—caveat: she was never to lift the lid. Of course the prohibition proved just too tantalizing. Like her sister Eve, discontent with restrictions that made no sense in the moment, Pandora lifted the lid, unwittingly unleashing pandemonium. A whole host of evils spewed out into the world. Yet one thing remained at the bottom of the jar—that precious essence, hope.

Does this tale mean to tell us we have to wade through layers and layers of curses in order to reach hope? Or does it mean that good and evil, blessings and curses are all mixed up together? The question is yours to answer, as it is mine. I go with the view that curses and blessings are entwined together, like chaff in the wheat, and thorns in the garden. Let's face it, this is not a tale with instructions about how to get back to innocence. The genie is out of the bottle and none of us can stem the chaos by slamming the lid back on the jar. Even if there were a way to do so, we would be clamping the lid on life's fullness, too. Can we take the evil without the good? No. Life, in all its beauty and terror, is a package deal.

Hope requires that we experience and participate in life's multiple-dimensions, not just in its pleasant aspects. To believe that we could fend off difficulty, deny the darkness, and find peace by clutching our little candle of hope away from the messiness of life, shielding it in a protective corner beyond the reach of the wind, is to deny hope its power. Hope must be brought to bear on life as it is.

Hope fills us with the strength to stay present, to abide in the flow of mercy no matter what outer storms assail us. It is entered . . . through the willingness to let go of everything we are presently clinging to. And yet when we enter it, it enters us and fills us with its own life—a quiet strength beyond anything we have ever known.[12]

# 2. HOPE DIFFERS FROM OPTIMISM

*When optimism dies, that's really when hope is born.*[13]

*A great deal of what is called hope in secular culture and popular religion is really wishful thinking, utopian fantasy, desire wrapped in illusion.*[14]

## HOPE'S EYES ARE WIDE OPEN

For hope to be worthy of its name, and not merely a positive outlook, it must embrace life whole, in all its multiple dimensions; "the bitter, the sour, the sweet, and the salty,"[15] and everything in between. Otherwise it is of no real help when the chips are down. Hope must have its eyes wide open to life *as it is*, because the way to the future begins with actual conditions in the present. "Play the ball where it lies on the field!" shouted our high school soccer coach.

I think of physicians who must relay bad news to their patients and who must find the artful balance required to do two things at once: deliver the facts, yet leave the door open for hope—a hope rooted in reality. Jerome Groopman, a compassionate physician and author, sees himself as an advocate of his patients' right to hope. And hope, in his experience, is not a trifling thing, but an essence that "has proved as important as any medication" he might prescribe, or "any procedure [he] might perform."[16]

No understanding of hope is honest unless it deals with the absence of hope and those seasons when nothing comforts or reassures. "I am allotted months of emptiness, and nights of misery are apportioned to me," lamented Job (7:3). While this example may seem overly dramatic, who among us has not shared, at some point, his experience of "tossing till the dawn"? It is human to be deeply disappointed and to encounter despair, and if we don't acknowledge this, and we expect ourselves to be always hopeful, hope becomes an ideal that is not human and a solitary burden. It fixes on "the sweet" and denies or leaves out "the bitter, the sour, the salty." It is a weak hope, unable to embrace life whole.

Living in the same neighborhood as hope, with its honesty and awareness of life's harsh dimensions, is optimism, hope's half sister. Optimism deserves respect, after all; it can provide the essential energy necessary to move forward. At times, we need to take refuge in optimism. When life delivers up bad news, we go to work revising it into something we can bear.

Optimism is right at home in a culture that idealized Horatio Alger. And here in America, optimism sells and brings in votes. Ronald Reagan was considered to be our most optimistic president. Athletic coaches are notoriously optimistic at the beginning of the season. So are candidates running for political office. You hear optimism's strains in their stump speeches; this or that problem can be addressed and solved if we will just elect him or her. Optimism appeals to the ego insofar as we like to think of ourselves as progressing. Even of hardship we sometimes say, "It was rough, but I learned so much through it all." That may be, but let me tell you, the idea that one is progressing, and the energy needed to find a positive spin, dies a thousand deaths in chronic illness, flattening optimism in its wake. One last point in optimism's favor is that it is far more energizing to be with a person who trusts in life and has confidence in possibilities, than with someone with a tendency toward gloom and doom, or who imagines the worst.

But optimism cannot sustain us, like hope can, in our darkest hours. It must constantly be propped up, with cheer, for example, or denial, or little pep talks aimed at the will. It cannot sustain us over the long haul. "Optimism tends to minimize the tragic sense of life or foster belief that the remedy for life's ills is simple." The hoping person, on the other hand, "has had experiences of fearing, doubting or despairing" and is "realistic about life and the obstacles to fulfillment."[17] This kind of person refuses to pretend things are other than they are. While someone without hope might passively rationalize or discount justice, the hopeful person stands against it and will not accept the status quo.

If we skirt around the edges of truth, fending off despair by refusing to see the present situation honestly, we ultimately shut out genuine hope, "if only because we cannot escape our own death or the spectacle of pain. . . . If hope is a bright indomitable bird, despair is the dark ocean over which it flies, against which it sings."[18] In optimistic America, hopelessness can be unacceptable to the point that it has to go underground. Repressed or denied, it runs around camouflaged, appearing under the guise of its many cousins: arrogance, overactivity, breathless cheer, cynicism, pessimism, impatience.

Considered in a compassionate light, both optimism and pessimism are strategies (conscious or not) for dealing with difficulty. Pessimism can snap into place as a protective device when we are suspicious that hope may be empty. Like cynicism, it seeks an alternative to a rose-tinted view of the world that does not square with reality. Drawing on psychological perspectives, optimism and pessimism might be seen as the equivalent of our bodies' immune systems that click into readiness when something threatens our health. This reflex, woven through our very cells, gives us the power to resist infection, fend off disease, and keep out foreign bodies. While the capacity to protect our vulnerabilities is essential, when our defenses congeal into a stiff, permanent state, they block out life's blessings.

Here is the difference between optimism and hope: hope is an essence that goes to the core of our common humanity; optimism is an attitude. Optimism tends to adopt the role of the spectator who surveys the evidence in order to infer that things are going to get better. In contrast, hope enacts the stance of the participant who gets into the fray and goes to work for change. This is critical from the standpoint of social justice, where hope will not settle for unnecessary suffering or sanction the status quo. Hope is able to envision something better and to move toward it with energy and resolve. Hope actively resists the status quo. It will not adapt to a situation that seems intolerable. It is discontent, and will be, until the situation is rectified.

We are living through a dark time in history, a time of cataclysm, when the breakdown of assumptions and worldviews we have held for centuries is made visible almost daily. Some say the changes we are living through are the most radical the world has ever seen. With this level of anxiety, it is no wonder we try to put on the brakes.

In the movie *An Inconvenient Truth*, former vice president Al Gore made note of a pattern among some who came to see and discuss his film about global warming and the environmental crisis we are in. He said what happens for some is that they wake up from their denial about this problem, but when they do, it is so overwhelming they move right into despair. Neither denial nor despair is a helpful starting place from which to understand the problem and work toward righting it. Hope exists in the territory between denial and despair. Hope has its eyes open to the problem, but senses a way forward, if only one step forward.

# 3. LIVING WITH A BEAST

*Tigers make a variety of sounds. They include a number of roars and growls, the loudest being most like the full-throated aaonh . . . a cry that travels far and wide, and is absolutely petrifying when heard close up. When they charge, tigers put out throaty, coughing roars . . . they hiss and snarl . . . grunt and moan. . . .*[19]

I h ave a chronic illness that rose up ten years ago with the violence of an unexpected, life-threatening animal wreaking havoc in my life. As I look back on it now, I see that this thing had been working its way toward me for a long time. For several years, I had various digestion problems that no one could figure out. Then came sleep disturbances and severe headaches. This was followed, in the fall of 1997, by dozens of symptoms that rushed in at once. I had the sensation of living in the same house as an aggressive Bengal tiger. (This seems to be an archetype we hold collectively. I swear my imagination offered it up to me long before I read Yann Martel's novel *Life of Pi*.)

At first, the creature emerged only now and then, elusively, like most wild animals, who are, ironically, both fierce and shy. Seemingly random symptoms floated in and out: terrible eye and head pain, photophobia, digestive difficulties, sleep problems, chest wall pain, glandular and jaw pain, weak muscles, excruciating exhaustion, buzzing and cold in my extremities, periodic dizziness, bladder problems, waves of fever, roving pockets of tissue pain, as well as arthritis-like symptoms. But the illness seemed to have no place to rest.

In the early days, I thought bargaining might be possible, and wondered how to defuse an enemy that had taken me hostage. Could it be lulled to sleep? Bribed or threatened, perhaps? As pain ricocheted from one place in my body to another in the course of a day, I tried lying very still to see if rest would help. Sometimes it did, but generally the symptoms kept up, and fear kept a choke hold on my thoughts, sending them leaping anxiously from one possibility to another; maybe I had Lyme disease, or something worse, a brain tumor or multiple sclerosis.

As I sat in my doctor's office on a warm September day, she leafed in puzzlement through her medical manual, tracing my list of symptoms, trying to untangle the knots. At one point, she mused aloud to my anxious ears: "One thing you do not want is chronic fatigue syndrome." No, I didn't. But I was clearly not in control here. As the illness gathered steam, it/the tiger said to me in countless ways, "You shut up. I am the boss here." It was not a question of him or me but of him *and* me. We were stuck in the same house together, and accommodating this "other" presence was non-negotiable. In fact, this intruder stalked me night and day, shadowing my every move, even the smallest, quietest, and subtlest. Just the slightest exertion of energy, say, by going to the grocery store and walking down three aisles rather than two, resulted in a crescendo of symptoms flooding back. I was like a prisoner, trapped within the walls of a narrow space. Hope backed up and huddled against the wall near the rear door, fear having robbed me of the courage to argue.

When fear was at its height, stirring up a constant panicky flutter in me, every life system on heightened alert, hope was the instinct to bar the door and mobilize every ounce of energy I had to keep the intruder out—if only that had been possible. I grabbed for the sandbags, piled them high against the door, planting both feet in such a way that all my weight could be given to leaning hard against it.

Hope was reduced to "hope nots." I hope this is not MS. (I had a friend die of multiple sclerosis in her early fifties, after years of confinement in a wheelchair, in a nursing home, being nourished through a feeding tube.) Oh please, God, not this. I hope this is not a brain tumor. (A high school acquaintance died slowly of one in his early twenties, despite heroic surgery after surgery.) Oh dear heaven, I hope not that. Nor lupus! (I remembered pictures of the southern writer Flannery O'Connor on crutches, her face puffy from steroids, dying from the disease in her midthirties.) Everything strained against these possibilities. There was not even the tiniest space to hope *for* anything. This was primal, stage-one, white-knuckled, bartering hope, bobbing on the whitecaps of dismay.

People said to me often in the early days, "Isn't it terrible to live with such uncertainty? Wouldn't you prefer to know what it is you are dealing with? To have a label?" Well, frightening as it was to be in the dark about the origin and true nature of this illness, it was better than the alternative—having some dread disease that was likely to cripple if not outright kill me in due course, but whose name was known. Given those options, I'd rather be in the dark and have a future. Hands down, every time.

I was shocked to be in such close proximity to the tiger. It took years of tests to determine that its bite was not lethal—though it sure felt that way. How could a person have so much pain, so many debilitating symptoms, and not need to be hospitalized? How could this complete system breakdown spell nothing—medically—wrong? When it lunged at me at all hours of the day and night, it was only mildly relieving to know it was not a killer beast. Kidnapped, reined in tight against my will, tethered to an animal by a short leash, I had little choice but to observe its habits, take note of its behavior, watch when it ate, when it rested, and what stirred its rage.

## TRYING TO BE A LEARNER

When symptoms persist, despite even heroic attempts to mitigate them, it may be that our psyche is trying to get our attention. In the early years, I was engaged full-time in managing pain. Yet even then, I was conscious that the soul has its own imperatives, often spoken through the body, and maybe my symptoms were messages sent to get my attention. This realization was fairly obvious, given that the beast kept intruding, crashing through the defenses I erected in an effort to bracket it, and stay *in* my life. What was confusing, however, was that I couldn't tell whether the force I was confronting was illness, my recalcitrant body, or my soul, and the messages it/they were sending. (As if they can be separated.) So I was not sure with whom to have a conversation, or at whom to be mad. What *was* clear was that the beast/illness would not engage in arguments. If I wanted to avoid creating a big scene with flashing lights and sirens, I needed to pay scrupulous attention.

To this day, my body continues to register its protests about overexertion and about any task that takes more than a few hours, or a schedule that makes for a long day. Sometimes I feel like beating the beast with a stick, especially when it pens me in a tiny cage. At other times, I see that these limits may be summoning my true nature to come out into the open, announcing, in no uncertain terms, that I am at heart a contemplative person who thrives on a slower pace than the active extrovert I have been. Quiet is soothing to me now, and solitude is welcome. Clearly my body has had to shout to get the attention of an achievement-oriented, people-pleasing, eldest child. A voice beneath my over-adaptive personality has registered its loud and long protest/request.

Illness forced a discipline of acceptance on me. Acceptance of severe limits, pure and simple. I didn't have to like it, but I did have to deal with this, one punishing blow after another, when I stepped across the line. The message was plain as day to see; my body and soul wanted regular rhythms of rest, underscore *regular*, like the ancient and revolutionary practice of Sabbath that I go around talking about, presumably because I teach what I most need to learn.

I had to pad each activity with periods of rest before and after. Like a delicate object, these pockets of health were so fragile they required the same level of attention and care given to transporting fine pottery or glass, with "FRAGILE" stickers plastered on all sides of the packing crate. One of the losses engendered by chronic illness is spontaneity, when every choice about the expenditure of energy is forced through the sieve of calculation. It flushes out joy, too, deflecting the energy that could be expended enjoying simple, everyday pleasures, to coping with aggravation and diminishment. Illness chews away at hope until it looks like flimsy paper decimated into tiny strips by a shredder. It also dresses down the ego.

Gradually, as western medicine came up short in my search for a diagnosis and help alleviating my symptoms, I turned elsewhere. Someone gave me the newsletter published by those who suffer from the same combination of symptoms I had, and suddenly this illness, and its complicated patterns, had a name: CFIDS, which actually covers three distinct conditions that can overlap: chronic fatigue, fibromyalgia, and immune dysfunction syndrome. A start, anyway.

There were times, early on, when I was tempted to blame myself for its incursion. After all, Chronic Fatigue, Fibromyalgia, Immune Dysfunction Syndrome (CFIDS) occurs frequently in active women between the ages of forty and sixty. Here's the truth of the matter. On one hand I *did* contribute to this illness, with my tendencies toward overwork, peddling hard to own a home and plan for retirement. On many occasions I have not honored my physical limits. Yet not everyone has suffered such penalties for these "offenses." That whopper of a message—that my lifestyle choices were *the* cause of illness—began to abate when I learned that the medical world had other explanations.

Numerous researchers believe CFIDS may be set off by a virus, and like a car engine idling at too high a speed, in those who suffer from it, the furiously spinning pistons will not slow down. They're frantic, running on high alert, like smoke alarms bleating continuously.

## TRYING TO REMAIN A LEARNER

Whatever the causes of CFIDS, adopting the stance of a learner has been a helpful coping strategy, a matter of self-preservation when a wild beast has you cornered. "The major difficulty in training animals is that they operate either by instinct or by rote."[20] So you must learn your animal's hunting patterns and figure out its hungers. Memorize what bothers it. Attend scrupulously to what it takes to get him to lie down. Like Pi, bringing the tiger, whom he named Richard Parker, fresh water and food several times a day, I followed my tiger's commands like a new recruit at boot camp. I renounced (temporarily, I thought) my former athletic, healthy self and my full-paced life, and stayed lashed to the beast. Ah, but renunciation did not stay renounced; I wanted to barter and bargain at every turn. But nothing doing. He was king, impervious to every remedy I tried.

As I said earlier, ours is a culture in which people have a lot of investment in putting the best possible spin on things. When asking about my health, others wanted to believe that I was progressing, too. But this is not a truth you can claim when you are mired in impasse, suffering under a big fat hurricane that is unleashing disaster through every aspect of your life.

The tiger/thief's basic message was "Obey me, or else." It had a hair-trigger temper easily set off. What seems cruelest about it is that the thing I love doing the most raised its hackles right away: being physically active. I used to be a runner, biker, swimmer, tennis player, skier, but when this illness descended, I could not have walked to the end of the block. I say this with humility, well aware that countless numbers of people have lost infinitely more than I have; their legs, their eyes, the ability to walk, even to eat. I have a friend in her early fifties who lives with a feeding tube because of crude radiation techniques thirty years ago that permanently damaged her intestinal track after colon cancer. She does not have the privilege of rolling a fresh summer blueberry around her tongue and of feeling that succulent fruit float down into her belly. My own losses dwindle in comparison. Still, they are losses.

I couldn't (and still cannot) always plan ahead, because it was impossible to predict what my pain or energy level might be. For a long time, I could not do anything before ten in the morning without suffering excruciating headaches and eye pain that stayed for days. Furthermore, just when I desperately needed sleep, insomnia descended. Or I would sleep twelve to fourteen hours and wake up feeling exhausted. If I was short of adequate rest even by minutes, pain came rushing back, pummeling me for days on end.

Eventually, after six or seven years, the cumulative effects of dozens and dozens of remedies (including homeopathic remedies), and the fruits of a gifted healer's help, little spurts of energy and strength began to return. This healer is a chiropractor by training, but that title does not adequately capture his intuitive ability to "read" the body's many systems, nor his wide range of knowledge about pain, nutrition, hormones, and the like.

There was more room to barter with the big cat. He was not so easily upset. Instead, it was as if he were camping out in an adjacent room and had other things to do than harass me night and day. Even so, if I stepped so much as inches beyond the narrow confines of the acceptable expenditure of energy, the result was a series of sharp electrical shocks that made me feel like I was the imprisoned beast. Is this what electric fences feel like to cattle, horses, and dogs? I wondered. A few harsh yanks on the chain have the same effect.

Thankfully, over the course of years, the tiger became somewhat less agitated. I could pacify him, temporarily, by resting often, stopping for hours between activities, sleeping long enough, and lowering my expectations for physical movement. Thanks to homeopathy, a whole regimen of supplements, migraine and pain medicine, eye drops, digestive and sleep aids, hormone help, and regular visits to homeopath and healer, I do have some weeks of strength, freedom from pain, and more energy. Even though they are not always reliable, I say, Hallelujah! Hope is able to take a longer view now. I have moved beyond coping hour to hour. Day-to-day life is less fraught with the turbulence of symptoms, though they are never far away. I must still carefully calculate what is possible and not possible. When I don't, the symptoms cascade back with a flourish.

# 4.  HOPE'S LIMITS

*Hope is not absolute in its range.*[21]

One of the most helpful sources of wisdom on hope for me has been the late William Lynch. A Jesuit priest, he was a chaplain at a mental hospital in Elizabeth, New Jersey, in the 1960s, surely a testing ground for hope. His insight is that it would be a misuse of hope to claim that everything can be hoped for. He's right. I, for example, am not going to be a tennis star. There may have been a window of opportunity for that forty years ago, if the circumstances had been right, but that window is closed now, and to hope for that kind of fame would be to distort hope, even to "contaminate" it.[22]

When hope is overly idealistic in a situation that warrants both hope and caution, it can be devastating. My sister Kathryn, a psychiatrist in Seattle, endured nine-hour brain surgery for an acoustic neuroma in 1994. Thankfully, such a tumor is usually benign, which hers was, though it leads, inevitably, to total hearing loss in one ear. It can also dramatically upset a person's sense of balance permanently, and it sometimes leaves drooping facial muscles and, thus, a radically altered appearance.

Kathryn's surgeon, a brilliant and tremendously gifted man, was able to repair nerves that were, in his words, "as thin as tissue paper," having been pressed upon by the tumor for what must have been years.

Unfortunately, he was not so skillful in his preparatory remarks to her. In a preoperative conversation about what she might expect, he told her that one of his patients had actually climbed Mount Rainier just weeks after the same surgery. Another patient, about Kathryn's age, had little trouble regaining her balance on a bike. While these testimonies were certainly true, they represented rare exceptions, not the general rule. Kathryn discovered, in a support group for people with acoustic neuroma, that many struggle through dizziness and disorientation, along with other losses and annoyances. It would have been far more helpful, even kind, to have painted a broader brushstroke, conveying the various outcomes for recovery across the continuum, offering her realistic expectations without taking away good reason to hope for the best possible.

Some of the most helpful words spoken to Kathryn in the recovery process came from a woman who had gone through life-changing surgery herself. She said to Kathryn, "You have to look at yourself in the mirror and introduce yourself to a totally different person than that of your former self, and get ready to live a different life than your previous one." To hold steadfastly to reference points from her pre-surgery life was not only unhelpful; it was deeply discouraging.

To live within the laws of the human condition is to bump up against constraints; it is to learn the difference between the possible and the impossible. While this difficult learning is daunting, it can also be freeing. Hope must come to grips with the present. It must begin with the facts and with what is possible. It may not end there, for it is every person's right to hope even for the impossible. But that cannot be its starting place.

The true locus of hope for Kathryn was in her capacity to adapt to a body with new limitations. It would have been fruitless, even tormenting, to have expected that she could do everything she had been able to do in the past, or to expect the complete recovery of hearing in an ear that was now deaf. A new body calls for a new self.

A person I trust as a voice of wisdom about limitation is Nancy Mairs, who has earned this trust through her honesty about the realities of living life in a wheelchair, with greatly reduced and ever-diminishing capacities brought on by MS. Mairs is wickedly funny, and in her book, *Waist-High in the World*, she shows that she has adapted graciously to the constraints of her disease. One of the unexpected results of living in a wheelchair is that Mairs is eye-level with people's private parts, a fact that tends to put everyone on the same level! Here is a sample of her buoyant attitude:

> On the whole, woe isn't me. I don't think I am, as the recovery would have it, "in denial." . . . I feel—and feel fully—the ordinary complement of negative emotions in response to specific triggers: anger and frustration at my clumsiness; embarrassment about my leaky bladder; wistfulness for the dancing and hiking and cycling I'll never do again; guilt that my helplessness burdens family and friends; anxiety about further deterioration. I simply don't feel especially sorry for myself. Neither do most of the other people with disabilities I know.[23]

Hope must work *with* the realities of her current circumstance. It cannot pretend that things are other than they are, or skirt around the present, because it is in finding a relationship *with* these realities that hope is needed. When your limbs move awkwardly, if at all, when they do not respond to your brain's commands, when simply getting dressed or going to the bathroom is a time-consuming undertaking that requires another person's help, hope's focus is on dealing *with* the situation at hand, *relating to it*, rather than against it. Hope's goal is to meet these hassles with a modicum of grace.

Finding hope enough to continue does not mean a person has to like her circumstances. Mairs is clear about the emotions that accompany having MS. "If rage and sadness are left unacknowledged and unaccepted," she writes, "they transmute readily into depressions. . . . Better, I have learned, to open myself wide to them, and then wider still, to permit them to sweep on through."[24] She does not believe MS has poisoned her existence. This amalgam of honesty, pluck, good humor, a gracious way of receiving help, and an ability to engage life as it is is remarkable.

Most impressive of all is that her illness has not closed her off to her true self, that dimension of her being that has not been crippled—either by disease or by any other life circumstance. In my own experience, the sheer coping that comes with constant pain, aggravation, and physical limitations has, for periods of time, closed me off from that self. I have found it difficult to access the wisdom and perspective carried by my "inner being" when I am tired, frustrated, and emotionally flattened by illness. I am sure Mairs has had her moments, but in general, she does not seem to "go there." This itself is cause for hope.

# 5. HOPE AND IMAGINATION

*Hope is directly related to the imagination. Hope actively scans the horizon for solutions and possibilities, for resources and perspectives. . . . Hope imagines, and it refuses to stop imagining.*[25]

The human imagination is an extraordinary faculty, vital to our well-being. One of the ways it comes to our aid is by posing alternatives, spinning possible routes out of difficulty, or offering a wider perspective on a problem. The imagination is central to hope in that it enlarges the present, linking current reality with dreams of what could be in the future.

While some people may discount the imagination, or equate it merely with fantasy and illusion, I side with those who speak of it reverently, calling it "the highest power of the knowing mind . . . prime Agent of all human perception."[26]

So often the roots of a word in different languages can shed light on its meaning. The German word for imagination is *einbildungskraft*. *Kraft* denotes power; *bildung* means shaping; and *ein* means one. "Imagination is the power of shaping into one, a wide array of truths and life experiences, enabling us to hold complexity and paradox together. Hope, and faith, by means of the imagination, are shaping, unifying activities that are integral to being human and to discerning the character of ultimate reality or eternal truth."[27]

We are not always conscious of the imagination's work. It is even on the job at night, when our will is at rest, in the form of dreams, which interpret, integrate, and reflect back to us the truth of how our psyche is experiencing life at the moment. Let me say more about its interpretive power.

## THE IMAGINATION AS INTERPRETER

Sometimes it is said that people create their own reality. What we mean by this is that how we experience something is largely a result of the way we see and think. This is true as far as it goes, but it is not true that people simply imagine the world into being, as though it does not already exist. It is more accurate to say that we compose that which we find, gathering it into the organizing template created by the broad array of our life experiences, filtering, filing, and framing it as we go. I want to anchor this idea with an example from my work as a spiritual director.

Often, when leading retreats, I begin by inviting people into a time of quiet, creating space in which people can listen to their lives for whatever may be stirring beneath the surface of their activities and obligations. As we settle in, I have a faint ripple of music playing in the background to help our busy minds slow down and to collect our scattered energies. After a few questions meant to focus their listening, I borrow an exercise from Ira Progoff's journal writing retreats.[28] The exercise encourages people to think of life as seasons, or "chapters" in a book. I ask in particular when "this chapter" of their life began. Maybe it began with a decision or an event. Or perhaps it coincided with a season in the natural world. After further reflection on their priorities in this time, I ask them to notice what comes when they finish this sentence: "This chapter in my life is like . . ." And what is it like? Is it like driving hell-bent for leather on a busy freeway trying to find the exit? Or is it like paddling a canoe, alone, on a quiet lake? Maybe it is like finding buried treasure, or the sudden blossoming of a garden after drought.

Invariably people come up with visual pictures or metaphors for this time in their lives without much effort at all. In fact, it's more accurate to say they receive them. Something glides into consciousness that is an extraordinarily accurate description of the person's current life state, internally. You can tell when this "click" happens by the look on people's faces when the metaphor or image is clarifying. It condenses a lot of emotional material into one frame. Whether they are surprised, relieved, or baffled, there's a sense, "Yes, this is truly how it is for me right now," and this awareness has a cathartic effect. The person feels more closely linked with her or his own inner truth.

I remember going through this exercise myself when I was having a rough time on the health front, and the image that came still resonates today. This "chapter" in my life was like a never-ending ride on a bumper car. Just when I got a little momentum going, I got hit from behind, then from the side, or the front, or still another direction. It felt like constant whiplash. My imagination drew a parallel between a ride at an amusement park in my childhood and my current state in illness, something my conscious mind might not have conjured.

What this exercise makes clear is that we do not just receive life as it comes; we also interpret it, shaping meaning out of the circumstances before us. My own imagination has been working full-time to interpret this seemingly endless siege with illness, on a level where emotional truth is not gussied up to seem better than it is by my overadaptive ego. Sometimes whole landscapes appear in my dreams; the land is brutally scarred, as if earth-moving machines had plowed into lovely fields and hillsides with indiscriminate force. In countless other dreams I am in prison, or searching at night for the nearest hospital. These images have the force of truth to them. They allow me to admit that illness has had this dramatic an impact on me.

## THE IMAGINATION'S POWER TO HEAL

To illustrate the imagination's remarkable power to help and heal, coming to our aid, at times, unbidden, I want to share a story. A man I know was sexually abused by his father beginning from the time he was very young. While he had worked diligently to move past those haunting memories and the devastating shame accompanying them, it all came roaring back every so often, yanking him into a quagmire of helplessness. He looks back on the dozen years that followed this abuse as blind coping, putting one foot in front of the other, focusing on his studies, on sports, and on music, trying to steer clear of his alcoholic parents as much as possible. Yet, remarkably, even as a child of eight, an instinctive interior wisdom was working on his behalf. He created, in his imagination, an alternate family with brothers, sisters, and different parents. He also pictured an imaginary tree house where he could retreat safely away from the trauma inside his household. Best of all, he imagined horses grazing just outside his bedroom window. Some days he even rode these imaginary horses to school.

The imagination clothed this man with images and associations that bore him up amid a chaotic family and sustained him by creating an emotional connection to a hidden wholeness within himself, even when his own family lacked the resources to do so. It revised his life story into something he could bear. Is this not grace? The psyche's spontaneous ways of gathering the interior resources we need for a given situation are a marvel. For this young boy, a secret family arrived on the wings of the imagination, and it happened without conscious effort. It brought him out from behind what might have become a prison of fear and shame; it carried him beyond the boundaries of his biological family. The imagination allowed him to experience life's goodness and to envision healthier relationships in the midst of what could have brought deep despair.

One of the most breathtaking tributes to this capacity in the human spirit is an eloquent portrayal of the imagination in the grimmest of circumstances. In 1996, Jean-Dominique Bauby, the forty-three-year-old editor of the French magazine *Elle*, suffered a stroke so massive it paralyzed everything but his left eye, the only muscle he could still move at will, along with a small degree of movement in his neck and head. This almost unimaginable frozen state is known as "locked-in syndrome."

Nonetheless, after he emerged from a six-week-long coma, a faithful friend of Bauby's devised a way to help him communicate. He made a letter board, placing each letter according to the frequency of its use in the French language. This friend, Claude, read off the alphabet with a pointer until Bauby stopped him, with a blink, at the letter that began a word. "This maneuver was repeated for the letters that followed," so that whole words and sentence fragments became a book, *The Diving Bell and the Butterfly*.[29]

Marooned in an old naval hospital in the seaside town of Berck, some days Bauby was rolled in a wheelchair into the main hall, where a stained-glass window depicted Napoleon's wife, Eugenie III, the hospital's patroness.[30] One day, Bauby imagined engaging Eugenie directly; he buried his head in the folds of her dress, and in his mind's eye, she encouraged him to be very patient.

On another occasion, Bauby imagined Eugenie joining him in his frightful state, even sharing his gallows humor:

> Not only was I exiled, paralyzed, mute, half deaf, deprived of all pleasures, and reduced to the existence of a jellyfish, I was horrible to behold. There comes a time when the heaping up of calamities brings on uncontrollable nervous laughter. . . . My jovial cackling at first disconcerted Eugenie, until she herself was infected by my mirth. We laughed until we cried. The municipal band then struck up a waltz, and I was so merry that I would willingly have . . . invited Eugenie to dance, had such a move been fitting.[31]

Here is the imagination at its most transformative, rising from the pit of even this crucible of suffering. Even here, on the shores of catastrophe, we see the marriage of memory and imagination at work, both of them handmaidens to hope. Bauby's imagination plucked one small detail, a picture of Eugenie in colored glass, and wove around it a story of gaiety, replete with dancing, which lifted him, if only temporarily, from the confines of a prison that would otherwise have been completely intolerable.

## THE COMMUNAL IMAGINATION

Bauby's story underlines the fact that hope is strengthened by interaction with the larger world. This is especially important when a person is isolated and alone. In our independent-minded culture, we may think of the imagination as a private resource. What happens, then, when the private imagination comes to the end of its resources—a well gone dry from the work of coping? What happens when we are exhausted and lack the energy for imagining? It is then that we must put on the imagination of another, or engage another person in conversation to kick-start our own hope. If we cannot find another person with whom to share our troubles, if we cannot engage life in some way, hope can be lost. Despair is about the shrinking of an individual's imagination. It means that something has become too much for a person, and his or her hope has collapsed in on itself. It needs the help of others to be revived. Remarkably, Bauby found a way to enter a relationship with a person no longer even living, and to find in it the means to go on. This is a tribute to the imagination's potency.

This is what friends, partners, families, and colleagues do for each other; they collaborate. Two neighbors lean across the back fence, pondering how they might help a troubled teenager on their block. A midlife couple, who have sickly, elderly parents, put their heads together to map a way through the difficult terrain of aging, the imagination coming alive in the exchange of ideas.

Our most intractable problems require community-wide solutions and the imaginative powers of diverse groups of people. The old adage, "A problem cannot be solved by the same consciousness that created it," is applicable here. There are examples galore of people coming together to pool their collective wisdom. From citizen advisory boards to political action groups, service organizations, book clubs, religious congregations, round-table discussions, town hall meetings, parent-teacher organizations, and neighborhood groups, all of them can foster a communal perspective.

## THE IMAGINATION AND OUR FUTURE

Hope for our world, and our precious planet, rests in large part on the imagination's power to extend our boundaries, stand in the shoes of another, and know that no matter how great our differences may be, we are one interconnected world. In other words, the imagination enables us to transcend the self, to awaken to others' plights and others' value, to want the good of others, and to love those outside our kinship circle. The imagination feeds compassion (*passion* meaning "to suffer," *com* meaning "with") and the ability to love in one another the diversity with which we are endowed. Our future depends upon this.

Traveling can extend our interest in and appreciation of others. So can reading, as well as watching the dances and movies and plays that originate in other parts in the world. An introduction to other people's art, food, clothing, educational systems, architecture, and business practices can help us understand and appreciate the uniqueness of other cultures. Friendships and partnerships that cross false boundaries can do this also.

The imagination's role on a societal, national, and global scale cannot be overstated. One of the most powerful attributes of the imagination is its capacity to pose alternatives. To propose life lived differently. Once again, our future depends upon this. Great changes are born in the imagination. In her grassroots efforts to curb development, in tandem with the people of Castle Valley, Utah, writer and environmentalist Terry Tempest Williams has learned that when people come together to imagine and collaborate, even across differences, community is created. "It is through the process of defining what we want as a town that we are becoming a real community," she writes.[32] We must imagine and devise means of transportation that do not rely on limited fossil fuels. We must envision ways to resolve conflicts that do not involve weapons. We must find the means to make a college education affordable for those of modest means. We must figure out how to strengthen public schools without threatening teachers or punishing students. The list goes on. In all of these efforts, the imagination is a remarkable and invaluable partner.

If, by means of the steady blinking of one eye, a seriously ill patient can find a way to endure the present in a suffocating diving bell, and if an abused child can be given a way to inhabit his own life despite the chaos and fear surrounding him, thanks to the imagination's gift of a secret family, it is clear that the imagination has its own extraordinary intelligence and serves as hope's handmaiden.

# 6. HELP—HOPE'S COMPANION

*Hope cannot be achieved alone. It must in some way or other be an act of a community, whether the community be a church or a nation or just two people struggling together to produce liberation in each other. People develop hope in each other, hope that they will receive help from each other. As with the imagination, we tend always to think of hope as that final act which is my own, in isolation and in self-assertion. But it is not this at all; this interpretation is, in fact, one source of its dubious and sentimentalized reputation.* [33]

One way to learn more about hope is to explore its relationship with its closest companion, help. People need each other. We cannot do life alone. Kids know this instinctively. "Will somebody tie my shoe?" the young child pleads, shamelessly, to whomever may be in hearing range. Children are masterful at making their needs known; skilled demanders, they plead for help at all hours of the day and night.

In Montessori schools, each classroom is comprised of several grades of children. The first, second, and third graders are together, as are fourth, fifth, and sixth graders. Why? Because the only way to negotiate the gifts and burdens of history is to do so in community. Trying to do this as a solitary individual is overwhelming and impossible. On the other hand, working in concert with others makes so much more possible. Younger children get to witness, firsthand, the accomplishments of older children, even as their own talents are welcomed and celebrated. They have the experience, on a daily basis, of solving problems as a group and learning that hope is inextricably bound up with help.

For those who believe hope is mostly an interior resource, I'd like to add a corrective. Hope has a private, interior dimension, to be sure, yet it's when our own interior resources are shot that we really need hope. Therefore, hope must rest in a sense that there will be help from the outside that can stir our own hope. In my own long struggle with illness, whenever I have felt there was something else to try, something that might offer help, whether it be medication, an alternative remedy, or the expertise of a healer, it has buoyed my hope.

Asking for help was and is not my first instinct. Like others in this culture, I too have been schooled to be independent and self-sufficient. This attitude has its benefits, which include taking the initiative to solve problems. An overextension of this tendency, however, can threaten hope.

## The Dangers Inherent in Not Asking for Help

People who work on mental health hotlines say it is when people isolate themselves from others that they are in most danger of suicidal thoughts and actions. Conversely, when they stay in contact with others, there is more hope for their continued life and health. Being alone too much, we lose both the perspective and correctives offered by community. Think of the times you have woken up on the wrong side of the bed in the morning in a foul or dispirited mood, but somehow, through the course of the day, in conversation with a colleague or someone at the grocery store, while listening to the radio, or hearing someone else's story, this mood changed. Somebody got you laughing. Another person's situation made you appreciate your own. Or engaging in necessary tasks made you simply forget about the problem.

## Help Is at the Heart of Our Communities

The tangible promise of help from the outside constitutes a primary thread in the fabric of our social/civil contract. If, for example, you were experiencing chest pains right this minute, and you dialed 911, or were rushed to the emergency room at the nearest hospital, a team of people you had never met, whose names you do not know, would immediately go to work on behalf of your life, even at great risk to themselves. This is a testament to the very best of our nature, and a cause for hope. It means we can depend upon each other. It means there are ways in which our care for each other, and our dignity as a species, finds expression every day. While this could be named a rather "secular" (as opposed to a religious) example, it personifies a central religious teaching, that God has committed us largely to one another's care.

Here is a story about the sacredness of help. A friend and colleague of mine, Pat Francisco, endured the nightmare that is every woman's deepest fear: being raped. Tragically, it is estimated that rape survivors in the United States number at least twelve million. What a shattering, sobering statistic. It puts my friend, sad to say, in a large company. But each individual rape is a tragedy beyond measure;

each one devastating and life-altering. Pat says of the "young time" in her life prior to her rape: "I was a young woman easily pleased, in love with her husband, and inclined toward happiness, unprepared for despair."[34]

Her husband was away on business for a few days that early summer morning when the rapist entered their South Minneapolis apartment. The violence continued for some time. In shock, when she was finally able to seek help from a neighbor, she was driven to a downtown hospital—a hospital she "would never have chosen." Hennepin County Medical Center was the downtown, county hospital. She had thought it "to be the facility of last resort, with a long wait and perfunctory treatment from a staff inured to suffering." Instead, she "was given exactly what she needed by people whose kindness seemed schooled by experience." The nurses and doctors seemed to know she was bereaved. Their voices were hushed. The lights were dimmed. "Men and women looked directly into my eyes with gravity and offered help," she writes. "The nurse on duty told me of the three rape survivors they'd treated already that morning."[35]

Yet in the tragedy and anguish of that experience, here was a grace note: if Pat agreed to call the police to report "the incident," she would not be charged for tests or services. The county would assume the costs.

> Something broke inside me when I heard this. From here forward, each time someone joined me in knowledge or action, it was as if a rope had been dropped over the cliff, offering a way up, a way out. The fact that the community would assume responsibility for my medical costs brought me back to the notion of a world I could belong to: a group gathered at the top of the mountain, furious enough to pay.[36]

## Asking for Help Can Be Difficult

Finding the courage to ask for help can be a last resort, arrived at only after trying every other option. When a person waits too long to reach out, her inner resources can dwindle, placing an impossible burden on herself as the sole source of hope. This delay can have tragic consequences. I am thinking here of illnesses worsening, depression deepening, or even the taking of one's own life because a person felt overwhelmed and alone. Hope is kept alive by an interplay between the person and the larger world, whether it be through relationships in a family, friendships, neighborliness, interaction with the natural world, or a relationship with God.

The power of receiving help notwithstanding, there are many reasons it can be hard to ask for help, and here are some of them. It feels like an imposition to burden another person with your needs. At the very least they have to take time out of their schedule and their own demands. There's the risk of rejection. Putting your needs out there exposes your vulnerability, scary territory for most of us, and certainly a threat to the ego, which wants to feel sufficient and in charge, not beholden to another. Receiving help can be disempowering if there are strings attached, or an unspoken expectation of payback. No wonder many recipients of charity have a legitimate fear of being controlled. This is why it is truly an art to give and receive help graciously and as equals.

It is the special talent of some to offer help with such basic needs in a way that preserves our dignity and enables us to receive it. Here, on yet another count, I turn to writer Nancy Mairs and the extraordinary spiritual feat she has accomplished in the way she relates to receiving help. She says of her wheelchair-bound life, "I view my crippled life less as a contest than as a project, in which others must participate if it is to prosper."[37] What a healthy way to "carry" her need. Listen to the way she links receiving help with caring for others:

> Permitting myself to be taken care of is, in fact, one of the ways I can take care of others . . . and I have to improvise these alternatives to the traditional modes of tendering care . . . since most physical acts are denied me, my efforts must take largely intellectual and emotional form. I've become a closer and more patient listener, and I spend time giving information, counsel, and encouragement. . . . Above all, I can still write, which for me has always been an act of oblation and nurturance: my means of taking the reader into my arms, holding a cup to her lips, stroking her forehead, whispering jokes into her ears.[38]

This is the utmost in living within one's limits without being emotionally crippled by them. I imagine it took considerable internal work to reframe help in such a way.

# 7. OUR HERITAGE OF HOPE

*We are our grandmother's prayers.*
*We are our grandfather's dreams.*
*We are the breath of the ancestors.*[39]

A s children, we absorb our parents' opinions, fears and anxieties, joys, preju-
dices, and worldview as naturally and unconsciously as we breathe in air.
Not only do we imbibe them; we live them. Their views simply are for us home
base, true north, our primary center of gravity. The way one generation engen-
ders trust and hope in their children enters first through the skin, through the
eyes and voice, long before it settles into our minds and takes up residence in our
language. "We are linked by blood, and blood is memory without a language."[40]

Along with the physical imprints that mark our likeness to our forebears,
our primary caregivers have also imparted meaning, reassurance, and comfort
to us through language, in the telling of stories, in the singing of songs and lulla-
bies, and in the way they responded to our endless litany of childhood questions.
One of the most formative powers elders have on their children, in the shaping
of hope, is the way they cope with disappointment, hardship, and loss. Children
watch these responses very, very carefully.

As we grow in age and maturity, more of ourselves comes into focus, the
governing past loses some of its authoritative grip, and we begin to size things
up for ourselves, holding our elders' views up to the light to determine what
we must revise, delete, amend, or throw overboard completely, in the service of
truth, as we see it.

If we are fortunate enough to have known our grandparents, we may be more
conscious of their ways of translating the world than we are of our parents'. We
sense as children that they, along with older aunts and uncles, occupy a much different place in our world than parents do. Their anxieties and opinions can differ
sharply from our parents', offering points of comparison. Even if their urgencies
and fears are not our urgencies or fears, or those of our parents, we take notice of

them. My grandmother had her cautionary lecture about germ-laden toilet seats, a topic I cannot remember my own mother mentioning even once. It was right up there on her fear meter with Communists. She was sure we would drown if we swam right after dinner, and that chewing ice gave you a stomachache.

## CAN HOPE BE PASSED TO THE NEXT GENERATION?

The tremendous power of family and primary caregivers in shaping their children's outlook on the world raises this question: Can we impart and pass hope along to the next generation? Or to anyone, for that matter—friends, lovers, spouses, acquaintances? I have often turned to Scott Russell Sanders's book *Hunting for Hope* in my graduate seminar on hope because he takes up this question in a memorable way.

This collection of essays, by a writer, professor, and father, begins with a confrontation with his son Jesse, then eighteen, when they were hiking together in the Rocky Mountains of Colorado. The tension between them was more than the predictable spat between teenager and parent. His father's worldview, with its attending lack of hope, had bothered Jesse for some time. Jesse felt his dad hated everything he liked—movies and television, music, billboards, snowmobiles, and Jet Skis. Finally, he let go with his pent-up rage:

> You hate everything that's fun. . . . Your view of things is totally dark. It bums
> me out. You make me feel the planet's dying and people are to blame and noth-
> ing can be done about it. There's no room for hope. Maybe you can get by
> without hope, but I can't. I've got a lot of living to do. I have to believe there's
> a way we can get out of this mess. Otherwise, what's the point?[41]

Had he really deprived Jesse of hope? Sanders wondered. What an indictment on him as a father! What an inheritance to bequeath! Did the price of awareness mean a sense of doom? Conscious of his role as a parent (of two) and a mentor to college students, Sanders made the commitment to intentionally search out reasons for hope as antidotes to all that seems wrong in the world. Jesse's cry was for hope in the here and now. That required a readjustment in his outlook. "Since I could not forget the wounds to people and planet," writes Sanders, "could not unlearn the dismal numbers . . . I would have to learn to see differently." Jesse deserved the first condition of hope, which is "to believe that you will have a future," and "the second is like it, to believe that there will be a decent world to inhabit."[42]

# Looking for Reasons to Hope

As he began to reflect on his own grounds for hope, he likened the exercise to gathering symbolic talismans for a medicine pouch. In the end, for Sanders, hope's primary sources came down to these: fidelity, skill, wildness, body bright, simplicity, and beauty. Of all these sources, I am most taken by the attribute of fidelity. I cannot think of anything more essential to my own sense of belonging and being cared for than the loyalty of my family and friends. They were the only balm in the worst days of illness. On this same note, each time I officiate at a wedding, I feel the need to say again what courage it takes to promise faithfulness to another person for a lifetime, when tomorrow is unknown, not to mention next year, or twenty, thirty, forty years from now.

Each of Sanders's themes deserves further elaboration, and I will take up several of them in the chapter on hope's sources. I want to share a story from my own family about the passing along of hope between generations. More than the telling of it, I hope to arouse your own reflections on your inheritance.

It goes without saying that each of us holds our personal history differently, yet I feel the need to name that caveat. Some of us found hope within our families. Others of us suffered from our family's inadequacies and had to go searching for it elsewhere in spite of them. Either way, you and I stand on the shoulders of survivors. We are the fruit of a million successes that enabled our forebears to survive and bear children, extending our lineage down through the centuries.

The historical times in which our ancestors lived, their geographical and social circumstances, their race and class, as well as their training and skills, had considerable bearing on their hope, whether they lived in comfort and plenty or in the shadow of poverty and loss. In many an "old country," but particularly in farm countries, families lived by the rules of primogeniture. The oldest son was generally the one who inherited the family farm, and if there were other sons, they had to find another way to make a living. It is here, in this predicament, that my own story begins. Whether there are common patterns between your story and mine, I hope that as you read you will consider your own heritage of hope and the multitude of factors that shaped your lineage and your own sense of hope.

# My Grandfather Leaves Norway

My paternal grandfather, Peter, was the youngest of six children and the second son. Consequently, when his older brother John assumed the farming responsibilities, he was sent to become a tailor's apprentice a few miles away, in the village of Molde, in the fjord country of west-central Norway. After completing his training at the tender age of sixteen, he was sent to America under the watchful eye of his rather gloomy and exacting older sister, Ingeborg, whose name itself, with its stiff, upright consonants that nearly bristle, pretty much describes her personality. Apparently, she was a commanding presence, who insisted that her brother wear a suit and tie at all times and that he have perfect posture. He would move out from under her clutches soon enough, free to choose his own behavior and manage his own life.

On the day of Peter's departure, his father, Aslak, escorted him out of the house and up to the orchard, where they could be alone for a final farewell. Though the exact words of that conversation have been lost, one could hazard a guess about the thrust of their exchange. Perhaps, in the manner of older Norwegian men, it was sparse on words but long on sighs, or even a few heartfelt tears. Yet even a taciturn father might become effusive on the eve of his youngest child's departure, unsure whether or not they would ever meet again. (They did not.) So maybe the emotion surrounding the moment unleashed an atypical torrent of words. Whatever the case, one gesture, thoughtfully conceived and gently offered by this father to his son, has not been forgotten. Its enduring imprint still ripples through our families' memories nearly one hundred years later.

Aslak thrust into Peter's hand a fistful of Norwegian silver coins and implored him never to spend this particular pocket of money, come what may. Whether he became a rich man, remained a relatively poor man, or rose to a more modest station in life, he was not to spend this money. Ever. That way, no one could ever call him poor; and no Norwegian father wanted to experience the shame of having only good wishes and no actual currency to offer. However, if money were the only gift he was able to bestow, that would not have been sufficient either. The coins were symbolic of the dignity and self-respect this father wanted for his youngest child, a hope that he would always be able to hold his head high. This physical reminder of the gifts inherited from his family would remain close at hand, jangling there in his pants pockets.

Shortly after my grandfather died of prostate cancer at the age of eighty, my grandmother pulled open the top drawer of the dresser in their cramped apartment hallway, jammed with furniture. There, among the jumble of note cards and address books, nestled on a square pad of white cotton in a jewelry box, were the Norwegian silver coins. That was thirty-five years ago, and I do not know where the coins are now. But their memory alone still does the work of hope. It reminds me that I am standing on the shoulders of people of meager means, who created full and meaningful lives on a foreign shore.

# How Is Hope Transmitted?

Just how did they transmit hope to us? For the most part, it was not shared verbally at all. In fact, I barely remember any conversation with this grandfather, though he lived until I was sixteen. What he and all my grandparents did was endure. They could not go back, really; they could only go forward, and they did, weathering hardship, bearing joy. They carried the years in their bodies. They absorbed and withstood a vast range of experiences: immigration, the Depression, war, illness, the loss of loved ones, satisfaction in their work, pride in their families, gladness in the company of friends, and tremendous artistry and creativity with their hands. Their lifetimes spanned a veritable river of history. And their memories held all their days together, under the roofs of their homes, the primary symbol of having made it in America.

Hope was not something they spoke of directly; it was embodied—in their habits of hard work and resourcefulness, in their silences. Its public face in them was endurance, the satisfaction of living with integrity, and their allegiance to honesty and humility. It was in the physical doing of things that they loved us, by fixing broken bicycles and repairing torn coats, making cribs for our dolls and desks at which to tend our homework.

# My Grandmothers

The grandmothers were more verbal than my grandfathers, and when I think of them I see a paradox. The one among them who bequeathed to me the most palpable and obvious hope was the one who had to struggle for it most, given her tendency toward melancholy. Given our heightened understanding of mood disorders today, I think she might well have been diagnosed with depression. Freda had to coach herself to see the good things life had brought and not overfocus on its tragedies. What this makes clear is that it's not necessarily the happy, cheerful people who give us hope, but those who have had to work for it. As her eldest grandchild, I was the beneficiary of her willingness to disclose herself to me emotionally.

She left Sweden at the age of nineteen, sailing for America in 1928, a solitary young woman, locked in her berth on the ship, wearing a small sign around her neck that announced she knew no English. She came to this country because her father, Erik, urged her to, having paid for her fiancé, George's, ticket two years earlier. Erik was an entrepreneur farmer, a joyful man with a love of adventure, who had come to the United States to work on the railroad in the early 1920s, and returned to Sweden with tales to tell and plenty of eye-catching money sewn into the lining of his coat. He told his second child that since she was engaged to

George, the son of neighboring farmers, it was her duty to follow him to the new country. And so she did.

Though she spoke not a word of English when she arrived in the United States, she had many family members in this country, all of whom had already made lives on this shore, working as maids, cooks, lumbermen, and carpenters; her uncle Charlie even ran a hotel. They were eager to welcome Freda and to help her create her own home among them.

When I think of her, Grandfather George, and my Neraas grandparents, Pete and Blenda, I marvel. Their modesty, minimal self-confidence, and public timidity belied the courage, pluck, and quiet doggedness with which they made very good lives. The astonishing abundance of skills they employed is truly remarkable. They literally built their own homes, made furniture, planted gardens, hunted and fished, baked, canned, and sewed suits and dresses, hats, slacks and coats, and matching Christmas and Easter outfits year after year; they knit, embroidered, crocheted, made draperies and blankets, created oil paintings, helped build a hospital and the Grand Coulee Dam, raised families, mastered a new language, struck up lifelong friendships, were generous neighbors, tithed to their churches, and had fun with friends and compatriots in various other circles of belonging.

There were formidable challenges and plenty of losses. My mother's parents lost an infant daughter in her first ten days of life. My grandfather's young brother was killed in a logging accident in southern Idaho. They dealt with ulcers, heart problems, and George's death at age sixty of heart disease. What they embodied, singly and together, was the capacity to live through the termination of one way of life and the beginning of another. (This is true not just of immigrants, of course, but of most of us.)

But the reason I felt closest to my grandmother Freda is that she let me in on her challenges and the ways she found to deal with them. I vividly remember her telling me about being a young mother when her husband was stricken with what they thought was spinal meningitis. Terribly frightened, she closed the door to the bathroom, got down on her knees, and prayed that George would live long enough to see their kids through school. Her prayer was answered. In her world, God was present, right in the middle of things. This God was not a chummy deity, but a transcendent Other, often elusive, and beyond our knowing, a power with high expectations of his offspring, but also, in her experience, a merciful presence to draw on. Asking for God's help was not saved for emergencies; it was a regular practice, day to day. I learned from her that a person is never completely alone. The most important gift she bequeathed was a larger context in which to see both suffering and joy. Call it trust or faith. Call it a spiritual worldview. What it offered her was a way to keep equilibrium internally, regardless of what was happening in the sometimes dangerous, sometimes shining, yet often unpredictable world.

Community was also crucial to her hope. She had many funny stories about neighbors helping each other through the lean years. During the Depression, when someone came back from the rationing table with two left shoes, they hunted all over the neighborhood to see if they could find their match. When a next-door neighbor brought over rhubarb pies, Freda and George sent back fresh fish that George had caught and vegetables from their garden. Hope was born, and kept alive, in these generous exchanges.

My family portrait would not be complete without a word about my parents. My father was a man with dreams, both for his family and for himself professionally, and he was willing to take risks on behalf of those dreams. With two young children and another on the way, he went out on his own as a young architect in 1957, one of Spokane's worst years economically. Happily, his practice is still thriving fifty years later. He has had ambition equal to his dreams, all of which have been exceeded. This has been due in part to the robust American economy, the privileges of race, and geographic circumstance. But his accomplishments are also a tribute to his energy and a willingness to take on most any project. There were lean years for sure; but all in all, his courageous choices, and my mother's skill at creating a lovely home with simple means, have been richly rewarded. Together, they have fashioned an endowment rich in hope for their family.

When I have faced risky decisions, the voice of this legacy has urged me to go ahead and make the leap. Even so, this voice has had to take into account the voice of my grandparents' generation, a cautionary voice that says: "Well, it may be better to hold back here; there is much to lose if you jump." Both voices have their place. Not only are fear and doubt woven through our inheritances; they are, along with honesty and clear thinking, hope's siblings, not her enemies, and hope is stronger for them.

## What about Your Heritage?

What has your own heritage wrought? Maybe you have found a way to birth hope in spite of your family. If that's the case, it may require a real mental stretch to name something of value bequeathed to you. That being said, it may be well worth the effort to ask yourself if there is not in fact something you inherited, something useful and close at hand, that you can draw on, like a handful of coins in the pocket, perhaps a wicked sense of humor, or an aptitude for hard work. What is hope's heritage in you?

# THE ANCHOR—SYMBOL
# OF HOPE

*Though the angry surges roll*
*On my tempest driven soul,*
*I am peaceful, for I know,*
*Wildly though the winds may blow,*
*I've an anchor safe and sure,*
*That can evermore endure.*[43]

H ere is an intriguing note in the history of human understanding of hope: the symbol used to represent hope by the early Christian community was an anchor. At first this sounds counterintuitive. To anchor a boat, or any kind of vessel, is to tie it down and restrict its motion. In contrast, the essence of hope is movement. It's a fluttering of expectation, a ripple of energy that leans into the future. Yet it is true than hope can steady a person. Hope was what grounded those first-century Christians in God amid the turbulence and persecution of the Roman Empire. Having to cope with that level of chaos, it must have been strengthening to know where their true harbor lay, and it was certainly not in the sociopolitical realm, nor in material well-being. It lay deeper, in a confidence that their lives were held in the embrace of a loving God.

Think of it this way: if something roots you deeply enough, a lot of movement is possible. When a person, community, or nation is well anchored in strong values and the support of others, it holds out the possibility of being able to manage two seemingly contradictory necessities—the need to hold fast when necessary and the need to bend when necessary. A deeply rooted tree can withstand gale force winds, though it may sway dramatically. Dropping anchor to stabilize your boat can free you to leave it for a while. You can get off and go explore the surrounding territory, go swimming, if that suits you better, or even lie on the beach with a book. Best of all, an anchor can actually do some of your work for you.

Anchors are usually, of necessity, rather heavy. The weightier they are, the more reliable, especially on the ocean, in dangerous tide zones, where double anchors may be needed; one at the bow and one at the stern. Heaving one over-board can require a capstan or the muscle of several strong men. My family has a place in the Pacific Northwest at the edge of the Puget Sound. We often watch, mesmerized, when monstrous oil tankers glide through our channel from Alaska, bound for the refinery in nearby Anacortes, their enormous anchors lowered and raised by huge cables. For smaller boats in relatively calm or shallow water, it can be enough for the anchor to simply rest on the ocean floor. But in deeper, turbulent water, the sharp ends of the anchor's flukes must dig into the sea floor to provide stability.

While hope has the power to anchor us, it has its vulnerabilities, too. It is a human virtue, after all, not a mechanical device, and Lord knows a dozen things can sink our little boat. I find it shocking, frankly, how quickly my own hope can evaporate, felled not by a large loss or a nagging affliction, but broadsided by something trifling and ordinary—a disapproving comment from a colleague who meant no harm or a dip in confidence as a teacher. Even a predictable event can throw us off. Our beloved neighbors of twenty-some years are selling their home and moving away. You know this experience. Something trips the wire, and what seemed at first like mild disappointment suddenly morphs into anguish, and you sink, unexpectedly. This ushers in the abrupt realization that something you had counted on, an enduring friendship, a professional role, or a talent at the center of your identity, actually served as a buffer, shielding you from a difficult truth. And there you are, feeling suddenly naked and exposed, while hope flies out the window, streaming hurriedly away as if carried by the jet stream.

When your boat is being pummeled by a choppy sea, how do you bind your-self to life? What are the anchors you throw out or the moorings you cling to? Are you anchored in someone's love? Do you reach for the familiar harbor of friends or the solace of a favorite place? Maybe you turn to God and know how prayer and meditation can still the anxious mind amid the swells of circumstance.

In the medieval world, the Roman Catholic Church translated the symbol of an anchor into a religious vocation. The practice of "anchorage," from the Greek word meaning "to withdraw," was a form of hermitage, widespread in Europe for several centuries. The anchoress or anchorite lived a life of prayer, cultivating rootedness in God away from the busyness of conventional society. The English woman Julian of Norwich, who lived during the Middle Ages, was just such an anchoress.

She lived in a solitary hermitage that was attached, like a small barnacle, to a larger men's monastic community, called Carrow Priory. The aspect of God's nature that was most compelling to Julian was God's accessibility, or "courtesy," in dealing with people. Julian's trust in God's providence was buoyed by the visions (or "showings") she received, visions that illumined the very nature and purposes of God. This gave her rock-solid hope in the general direction of life and in the ultimate fulfillment of the Creator's designs. She could say with confidence: "All will be well, and all will be well, and all manner of things will be well."[44]

This is no romantic notion, based on a rose-tinted worldview, but a bold statement of faith with no conditions. She did not say all would be well if people prayed hard enough, or all would be well when the plague was over, or all would be well when a new king came to power. She said simply: "All will be well." This is not inevitable hope; heaven knows the problems in her time were just as frightening as many contemporary problems are now, and she saw too much to be optimistic. The hope she experienced was always counter to the status quo, just as Jesus' hope was grounded in the sovereignty of God, not in the government of his time.

Julian's rootedness in God made her an anchor for others. Historians tell us that these hermits were often consulted, through the small barred windows or revolving hatches of their cells, on matters both holy and commonplace. One might imagine that Julian's seclusion was frequently punctuated by townspeople, who came to her with their sorrows and troubles amid the storms of politics or poverty. Perhaps she welcomed them with such hospitality, and had such a steadying presence, that they felt warmed, despite the cold stone room and bone-chilling English winters, and left feeling whole and hopeful again.

# 9. BORROWING HOPE

*Our friends hold our essential character for us.*[45]

The summer I was eight and my younger sisters six, five, and two, we took swimming lessons at the public beach on Hayden Lake, in northern Idaho. It was, and is today, a beautiful, peerlessly clear mountain lake fed by an underground aquifer. Some parts of the lake are so deep that the bottom has never been found. It's a good thing I was unaware of this at age eight. I had troubles enough managing my fear of being caught in tall forests of seaweed and large, ugly fish that lurked in the depths waiting to "get" me.

Since I was the oldest, my group's lesson was the first one each day, and its price was swimming when it was still rather cool on those early June mornings. I remember a lot of shivering, and I mean the shaking kind, where I huddled in a towel with goose bumps, knocking knees, and the attending blue lips. But the benefit of going first was being able to lounge on the sand with my mother and infant sister while Kathryn and Nancy, ages five and six, had their lesson.

I vividly remember the day the beginners' class faced the test to see if they could move on to advanced beginners. The requirement was keeping their head under water for long enough to sink to the sandy lake bottom, grab two fistfuls of sand, and pop upright again, with both hands in the air. Performing this feat was a huge step along the various ladders of childhood. A long line of preschoolers waded out into the sandy cove together, holding hands, until they were about waist deep in the water. Then they turned to face us and their teacher, who stood closer in, about knee deep in the shallows. She alternated between barking instructions and punctuating them with a shrill whistle, adding to the fear of the already anxious.

The whole long line of kids sank beneath the surface in unison like a loose string of beads, some hesitantly, others at once and without delay. Well, all but one of them did. My sister Nancy was much too afraid to get her head wet. She hesitated there, in the manner of young children, caught in the tug between fear and pride. Fear, in this case, had the stronger hand. Meanwhile, Kathryn, the elder of the two, sank to grab her fistfuls of sand, but just as she surfaced, she saw that Nancy had not dipped down. She was still standing. Quickly, in the primal, split-second reflex of one sibling diving to bail out the other, she handed over some of her own sand to Nancy, then, belatedly, held her own hands aloft.

This gesture took place very quickly and had a tenderness about it that was quite natural to Kathryn. I have always thought it among the kindest gestures I can remember from childhood, though surely there were others, exchanged unselfconsciously in the give-and-take of growing up.

If you can borrow from another person's bounty to win yourself a little more time to manage fear, surely you can borrow hope for a while, until that time when you have what it takes to brave the elements and fish around in the depths for your own. Like a loan, you take temporary use of another's resources, but you trust there will be a way to make it your own someday.

## LEANING ON ANOTHER PERSON'S HOPE FOR YOU

At times, it can be easier to have hope for another person than to have it for yourself and your own situation. About a dozen years ago, a friend of mine suffered in ways that threatened to totally undo her. She awoke to remembering childhood abuse through memories long repressed. And for good reason. Both parents had sexually abused her. They were successful leaders in their political party and church, and denied anything of the kind, which made it all the more insidious. The way back to a safer shore for my friend was treacherous and daunting. At times, the darkness was so overpowering she was not at all sure that life was worth such trouble. This was total shipwreck, a menacing danger that left her feeling like she was drowning, with no felt sense of the possibility of land.

Nevertheless, after months of work together, her gifted and compassionate therapist began to see genuine movement in my friend. She had finally found and claimed her anger, a sure sign of self-love and self-respect. There were small but growing pockets of time in which she could sleep without nightmares, and other telltale signs of hope. Healing was threading its way, inch by incremental inch, through her psyche and body, though she could not yet see or feel it. The therapist proposed that my friend borrow hope from her for a while, until the day came when she could take it into herself enough to be warmed by its flame. In essence, she threw her client a buoy and my friend grabbed on. We put patients on respirators, after all, so they do not have to expend extra energy breathing on their own while their body responds to other crises. The machine does the breathing until the patient is strong enough to do so on her own.

When I think of borrowing hope, I think of physical therapists who help lead people back in the direction of mobility and strength after life-altering accidents or strokes. Their clients must literally lean on them even as they lean on railings, bars, crutches, and walkers. They have a sense for the arc of the healing process over a long period of time. Because they have quite literally seen it all, they tend to be honest, not prone to overly optimistic idealizations. They are sources of believable hope for their clients.

This is hope related to help. Too often, in a culture rife with the illusion of self-sufficiency, it may be forgotten that hope depends in large measure on our access to resources and our embeddedness in community, or the trust that when interior resources fail us, or are lacking altogether, there may be external resources that can kick-start us.

In the worst days of my own long illness, I well remember a dreary Saturday morning in late winter when my friend Carol came over to be alongside me for a few hours. I was near despair about another relapse, lying prone on the sofa drinking tea. I was feeling what Emily Dickinson said of pain, though I did not have the words at the time:

Pain—has an Element of Blank
It cannot recollect
When it begun—or if there were
A time when it was not—[46]

Carol listened to my lament for a long while, sharing my discouragement, bitterness, disappointment. Later, when I had come to the end of my complaint, she wove a bridge between despair and hope that I could walk across. And what stepping stones formed the walkway? Gentle reminders of specific instances when I had been somewhat better. True, they may have been subtle, but the shifts were noticeable. "Remember?" she asked. "You were able to walk two blocks to the lake, for the first time, just weeks ago." Chronic head and eye pain, dizziness and fever, glandular, jaw, and chest wall pain had partially subsided. Excruciating fatigue was far more mute. "The illness has temporarily stalled," Carol suggested, "like a stubborn storm. The tornado has wreaked tremendous havoc in you, there is no denying that, but in general it is working its way out. Notice the things you can do that you could not have done eight months ago." She was right. And that metaphor meant everything to me. The storm had stalled.

Had she lobbed cheery nostrums over the fence from a comfortable distance, without joining me in the valley, her words would have felt not only rude but cruel. Grief cannot abide high-pitched cheerfulness. Or had she cut me off from my own necessary lamentation, I would not have taken in the truth of what she said. She did what friends at their best can do—be present, listen, and attend, yet stand outside our own pain. Pain over time can make us muddled, inarticulate, and fuzzy-headed. It's hard to know what is true anymore. "Pain—has an Element of Blank." But friends know our lifelines. They have witnessed our patterns of action and being. They can mirror back, realistically, things we cannot see ourselves. Carol had earned the trust necessary for me to borrow hope from her. It cannot be borrowed from just anyone. Those too naive or romantic, too sentimental or cheerleaderish will not make the grade.

Carl Jung said that in depression we do not see very well. The same could be said of chronic illness. After a while, it seems like one long slog through an endless swamp, without beginning or end. The terrain has a lugubrious sameness. It feels like it has always been this way and will always be this way. There are no landmarks anymore. No helpful reference places that show your progress, like the street markings in a marathon: "Oh, there, mile twenty-one! Thank God, I'm almost there, only five miles to go!" That's why we may need help to see.

The image of a storm passing through was food somehow, sustenance enough to live on for at least some days to come. "I AM NOW IN A STORM," I kept saying, or "A STORM IS IN ME." In fact, I've been pummeled, buffeted, and drenched. The levees have burst. I feel like I am going under. However, there are signs that this dangerous weather pattern is not going to camp on my doorstep forever. It is actually moving (though it's taking years). And the symptoms it is unleashing in me are not as debilitating as they were previously. Plus, there have been increasingly lengthier interludes of clear weather between squalls. Is this any comfort to a person in the midst of a hurricane? Yes, actually, it is.

Borrowing hope has a number of variations. Sometimes we borrow it from those who know the terrain that we are in. Or we borrow it from someone who may not have experienced our situation exactly, but she or he knows from whence we have come and can say with all sincerity, "You are here" on the map, and "See how far you have come." This is precisely what my friend Carol had done.

Then there are stories, or metaphors, that bolster hope because we intuit a truth we need through them. They can touch us at an unconscious level in a way that refocuses the lens through which we see our situation.

In a chapter to come, I will explore the way one particular story served this purpose for me. First, however, we turn to the ways we can choose hope as an inward stance, whatever the outer circumstances.

# 10. HOPE AS A CHOICE

*Not knowing when Herself (the Dawn) might come—*
*I opened every window.*[47]

*To hope under the most extreme circumstances is an act of defiance that*
*...permits a person to live his or her life on her own terms. It is part of*
*the human spirit to endure and give a miracle a chance to happen.*[48]

I am able to relay the following story only because Gail Milstein, a student in my Literature of Hope class, in the spring of 2004, interviewed Patty Wetterling and granted me permission to share her responses here. Gail felt particularly close to Wetterling, though they had never met in person before the interview. Gail gave birth to her first child, Sam, the same autumn in which Jacob was abducted. The Wetterling boy disappeared on a Sunday evening. The following Monday morning, as news reports flashed details of this tragedy, Gail nervously handed her three-month-old, Sam, to a daycare provider and went back to work after maternity leave. She and her husband have parented their three children in the shadow of the Wetterlings' loss.

Patty Wetterling is a Minnesota homemaker who has had to carry a grief that no mother or father should ever have to bear. A slight, sandy-haired woman in her early fifties, she lives with her husband in the quiet community of St. Michael, Minnesota, about sixty miles west of the Twin Cities. Their son Jacob was abducted by a masked gunman in 1989, at the age of twelve, while riding his bike to a grocery store on a Sunday evening with his brother Trevor and friend Aaron. Neither Jacob's body nor any article of his clothing or clue to his whereabouts has ever been found, though search teams tirelessly scoured the area for months and years.

What happens after the initial shocked panic, when the fluttering of anxiety wears off, and year after year goes by without any tangible reason for hope? Do the icy fingers of hopelessness lock, frozen, into place? Surely they could. On the other hand, maternal and paternal adrenaline might feed hope. After all, "there is an authentic biology of hope,"[49] just as there is a biology of fear and anger and anxiety, and belief and expectation are its key elements.

Patty Wetterling is not without hope in regard to Jacob, though I am sure she has had her moments. Publicly at least, she has channeled her grief and rage into work as an outspoken public advocate for families of missing children. Cofounding the Jacob Wetterling Foundation with her husband, Jerry, in 1990 "to educate families and communities to prevent the exploitation of children," she has reached out to dozens of families across the country. She is no longer a quiet woman out of the public eye, but a leader working on behalf of kids and a safer world.

Well aware of the statistics, she knows that after this much time has elapsed, it would be an almost inconceivable miracle to find Jacob alive. Still, she cleaves hard to another possibility, choosing, consciously, to hope. This is a testament to the love of a parent, and an acknowledgment that in the broad terrain between outright denial and naive hope, there are quiet truths to be claimed. She will not surrender her right to hope that somehow, someday, her beloved boy will walk through the door.

When speaking about her four children, she names each of them, along with their current ages, including Jacob, who is now, in her mind, twenty-six years old.

This is radical hope. Hope in the face of a firing squad. Hope in the face of the facts, of overriding evidence to the contrary, of having not the slightest clue how it might be realized, but choosing hope nonetheless.

Wetterling's connections with other parents of missing children have enlarged her hope, amplifying and expanding it beyond her own family, to a broader hope for humanity. This is what grief or pain can do—move a person out of past personal pain into the collective pain of the human family.

Patty Wetterling has adopted a bold stance toward her son's abductor. From time to time she screams at him, whoever and wherever he might be. "You are not going to take anything more from me than you have already taken!" she shouts. "You cannot have my marriage. You cannot have my other children. You cannot have my hope or my faith. And you are absolutely not getting me to buy into the attitude of 'stranger danger.' I am sorry, but if my kids never meet another stranger, they will never meet another friend."

This attitude has been hard-won. Several days after her son's disappearance, she crawled into bed, pulled the covers over her head, and said to herself, and whoever else might be listening, in the vast expanse of her grief: "I am not moving from this place; this is just too hard to deal with. I can't do it." Not many moments thereafter, she had "this vision, this really clear image of Jacob, curled up in a ball the same way I was, saying the same thing: 'I can't do this. It's too

Jacob, who is now, in her mind, twenty-six years old.

This is radical hope. Hope in the face of a firing squad. Hope in the face of the facts, of overriding evidence to the contrary, of having not the slightest clue how it might be realized, but choosing hope nonetheless.

Wetterling's connections with other parents of missing children have enlarged her hope, amplifying and expanding it beyond her own family, to a broader hope for humanity. This is what grief or pain can do—move a person out of past personal pain into the collective pain of the human family.

Patty Wetterling has adopted a bold stance toward her son's abductor. From time to time she screams at him, whoever and wherever he might be. "You are not going to take anything more from me than you have already taken!" she shouts. "You cannot have my marriage. You cannot have my other children. You cannot have my hope or my faith. And you are absolutely not getting me to buy into the attitude of 'stranger danger.' I am sorry, but if my kids never meet another stranger, they will never meet another friend."

This attitude has been hard-won. Several days after her son's disappearance, she crawled into bed, pulled the covers over her head, and said to herself, and whoever else might be listening, in the vast expanse of her grief: "I am not moving from this place; this is just too hard to deal with. I can't do it." Not many moments thereafter, she had "this vision, this really clear image of Jacob, curled up in a ball the same way I was, saying the same thing: 'I can't do this. It's too hard. They're never going to find me.'" She began, immediately, to talk to him. "Hold on, Jacob, stay strong," she yelled, in a voice growing bolder, in the determined if desperate manner only a terrified parent of a missing child can know. "We will find you." At that point she made a very conscious decision to get out of bed. Even now, all these years later, she says, "It is hope that gets me out of bed every day. It is a very conscious choice." A mother and father have the right to their hope, even in the face of official facts and probabilities.

Wetterling bears witness to the truth that hope is created in community. She speaks of help that has arrived from all directions—from law enforcement and the media, and "from every religious denomination imaginable."

"The world wants to hope," she says. "But we are so factually based that when you look at the facts, it does not seem at all hopeful. But I think that by nature people want to hope, and they want to help. In some ways, our family has been the benefactors of others' hope and help, and in some ways we offered them something they needed, too, a way to help. So we both won."

How does she adjust to living without an answer? To be truthful, she says, she does not know. Yet her own instincts to reach out, and the energy that comes from being proactive, have softened the hard reality that there are no answers to questions about Jacob's whereabouts. She has found great strength in the collective energy created by other families who have lost children and who understand each other's heartache so well. She has also been a leader in calling for legislative changes around sex offender registration laws. She has a fierce commitment that comes from knowing what she is fighting for—children's safety and a reduction in the number of missing and sexually exploited children. "You cannot steal kids," she says. "It is just wrong."

What advice or wisdom would she offer to strengthen the hopes of other parents waiting without answers? She suggests that the opposite of hope is fear:

> I dare to believe; I dare to have the courage to believe, to hope. It takes courage sometimes, because you might be wrong. All right. I was living this life that I believed in, and somebody took Jacob. And that world shattered. Everything. And then it came to that decision, to tell the kidnapper that's all he gets, that's it. It's a battle between me and him. And I refuse to let him win. And I have just dug my heels in. . . . I deal with others' fears a lot because so many people see me and they are scared. They grab their other children! But I've researched this for a long time, and there is no research to show that scared kids are safer and that scared parents are better parents. So I would rather see parents latch onto what they want the world to be and fight for it and don't let our fears of all the bad stuff win. I had to redefine myself. I had to redefine everything. There are a lot of people doing amazing things out there, and I find hope in that.

This kind of hope simply knocks me out because it is hope willing to gamble. The sheer force of love exposes (in this case) a parent's (or a lover's) vulnerabilities, and leaves her at risk of further heartache, but she risks it anyway. It is a way to claim the truth that something that makes sense spiritually does not necessarily make sense psychologically. Wetterling could have turned inward, shutting out the world and assuming a protective posture. She chooses another way. She claims her right to hope.

# 11. MATURE HOPE

*One of the qualities of hope is that it's not a one-day show . . . hope extends over time. And action that proceeds from hope means that if your choices are not the choices you'd like you don't say, "Well, I did my thing, I voted—once." And go home. You come back the next time and the next time, and you become a force that is clear in American politics.*[50]

In the days following September 11, 2001, as I began to let in the consequences of the evil actions unleashed on American soil, I kept asking myself who I wanted to be within this storm. Whose wisdom and worldview could take in this horror *and* find a way to hope at the same time? Whose particular company might offer both solace and the fierce, clear-eyed seeing that I was seeking in those days?

I thought of the moral giants of our time, people who live nowhere near Minnesota, but whose being alive in the world was comfort in itself; the writer and Nobel Prize winner Toni Morrison; the prophet/priest Dan Berrigan; Joan Chittister, OSB, an outspoken writer, speaker, and Benedictine abbess. Jimmy and Roslyn Carter, whose diligent work toward peace, whether by overseeing elections in newly emerging democracies, building houses for Habitat for Humanity, or engaging in mediation work through the Carter Center for peace, makes me proud to be their fellow citizen.

Closer to home, my thoughts led to a beloved rabbi in our community who is wise, kind, and gentle in his love of people, a *mensch,* to borrow a Yiddish term for a sage. I thought of several remarkable nuns I know, stupendous human beings, who are intelligent, witty, and discerning. Best of all, they abound in humor—which contributes to their staying power. I admire their commitment to justice and their willingness to rock the ecclesiastical boat.

Their stature as truth-tellers and courageous risk-takers has come from a willingness to direct their incisive critiques about abuses of power at the ruling powers of their day. In a culture of deceit and half-truths, their honesty is inspiring, though threatening to some. They have seen too much to be optimistic, yet they harbor the outlook and attitudes that make for genuine hope. These are people keenly aware of life's beauty and its savagery, yet they have such nobility of character that to be in their company is to find a presence that shelters. What they share is a depth of consciousness that is counter to our culture's enthrallment with the material world and our eagerness to assuage the appetites of our little local selves. They lament, grieve, and celebrate like everyone else, but theirs is a quality of consciousness and hope that is aware of an interconnected universe in which no one is free or well until all are free and well. They inspire confidence that we humans are capable of bearing a great river of truth. Or, better said, that this same river courses through us when we are available to it. Theirs is a quality of hope that "does not come at the end, as the feeling that results from a happy outcome. Rather, it lies at the beginning, as a pulse of truth that it sends forth."[51]

A hope that stays at the fix-it level, wrapped around the individual ego, is terribly fragile in comparison. Since life is fraught with inevitable change, uncertainty, and misfortune, if hope is tied only to the rise and fall of the ego's dramas, it will inevitably crash. While we know this intellectually, the "little self" in us can still make claw marks everywhere, trying to manipulate, desperate to control.

As my memory cast out its lines in the days after 9/11, trying to draw into my consciousness those who embody mature hope, I kept circling back to a group of older women—grandmothers, most of them, and long-time members of an inner-city congregation where I was once a minister. One particular hour I spent in their presence has stayed with me years later.

On the day the verdict was read in the trial of a public figure accused of killing his wife, I was driving to a lunch-time meeting at their church. Just as I turned into the parking lot, the radio announcer said the accused had been acquitted, after a protracted trial. As I walked in, there were the old women, as they have been on hundreds of Tuesday mornings, in the parlor, a huge, drafty hulk of a room, large enough to double as a gym on other days. They were bent over a large square table, sewing. Or was it knitting? No, it was sewing. They were sewing up the morning with their needles, sewing their compassion into yet another quilt for a needy recipient, sewing up their worry in the skein of routine, sewing up the fruits of lifelong friendship. They spoke quietly among themselves. Once in a while a soft chuckle would erupt, or a request be made to pass the coffee. These women knew each other so well, having shared a lifetime of sewing circles, church gatherings, shared joys and losses, that they purred like cats in the familiarity of each other's presence.

I recognized their distinct voices. There was Mary's slightly bossy tone, rising above the others as she named the week's prayer concerns and reminded everyone to bring birthday cards the following week. Then there were Sally's lighthearted rejoinders, which tempered Bertha's sometime stridency, and there was Caroline, going deaf at ninety-four, asking from time to time that certain lines be repeated.

I was fuming as I entered, put off by our legal system. Yet no one batted an eye, let alone reacted to my fuming. There was simply this slowly delivered line from Josephine: "Well, he's not gonna outrun justice in the long run, dear." Her comment made me think of Brother Martin's, when he said: "The long arm of history bends toward justice." A mighty long arm, one would have to say. "The Lord holds the world," Jo continued. "By and by God will put things to rights."

If nearly everything that can happen to people does happen, these old women, together and alone, had been through most of it and were not easily moved. They had borne difficult sorrows and met with many a storm. One had lost a grandson in a gunfight; another had recently lost her son-in-law to cancer; several had kids or husbands who had spent time in prison; one was living on her daughter's donated kidney. Most of them lived on precious little money. Several had been the targets of racism. Having lived through so much, they had little patience with lies or quick fixes. Yet each had a jovial side. They barely reacted to that day's news because they have *never* been able to put all their faith in the short term; they have always had to take the longer view. "The more mature the life, the larger is the time range and the scope of ideas and intentions within which a person lives and breathes," wrote William Lynch.[52]

Their trust in the fulfillment of large hopes is far from passive. They have managed the church's free store for years, brought food to the sick and tended the brokenhearted, staffed the Sunday school and served lunch at funerals. Steady, rooted, discerning, practical, yet ready with a dash of irreverence, they personify mature faith and mature hope. They were the solace I was seeking.

## MATURE HOPE IS STILL HUMAN HOPE

Being a person of mature hope does not mean you do not simultaneously feel discouraged or even bitterly disappointed. Nor does it mean you can simply sail over your hopes related to daily life, here and now, and discount them. That would be spiritualizing hope into a lofty, rarified ideal. On the contrary, hope is a living, pulsing reality alive in the particularities of people's real-life circumstances. To deny that you have a specific hope because it might seem selfish, or common, "can . . . create a perilous divide in consciousness."[53] This tendency to discount or undercut our desires is a particular liability for women. It is a reminder that hope is intricately bound up with truth. "The soul is bound up with honesty in some way that cannot, except at great cost, be violated."[54]

My own honest truth is that I want strong, steady health. As much as I wish I could either transcend illness, jettison above it, bracket it, look past it, or pretend I do not want it, when I'm in a trough of pain and debilitation *yet again*, there is no distance between me and my hurting body. The content of hope in these times is health and freedom from pain. Period.

I would wager a bet that even if the likes of Buddha, Moses, Jesus, Muhammad, or a bodhisattva herself were suffering severe eye pain, she or he would stop everything else and work like mad to deal with it. If there is anything I have learned in years of chronic illness, it's that I must stay true to my path, must claim hope in my own way. This means not pretending. I am already too well schooled at pleasing others and sparing them any possible burden by pretending that I am just fine. Enough of that already.

## EVEN HEALTH IS TEMPORARY

When you are on the underside of a cliff and you have tried countless ways to find a toehold somewhere—anywhere—to scale the sandy wall, your wholehearted focus is on any possible ridge that might support a foot and the remainder of your weight. When the sand and shale spill down over your head and eyes, and it seems there is no toehold, then you look around for the possibility of a tree limb to grab on to. Nothing more. There is no way, in that moment, to step back and take the forty-thousand-foot view. Everything is focused on the nearest branch. If and when the branch of a tree is in your clutches, however, and most of your weight has been heaved over the ledge, if somewhat awkwardly (your bum over the precipice at least, though both legs still dangle over the edge), a new realization appears. This branch, while lifesaving, is only a branch, a temporary help. It is not strong enough to support hope long-term. I am obviously referring to my quest for physical health here.

Invisible jewel in the crown though health be, blessing among blessings, it is ultimately fragile, not something we can claim once and for all. This is not nihilism or gloom, but God's honest truth. These bodies of ours may take us to the gate of the next world, but they will not take us through it. And even if you or I are enjoying mostly steadier health, what about the millions of other people still underneath the cliff?

It was Søren Kierkegaard who said we must hold to life's blessings as we would hold a thistle—cradling them without grasping too tightly, since overattachment can cause suffering. This is *the* insight central to Buddhism; everything is impermanent and constantly in flux. This has implications for health as well. Jewel in the crown though it may be, to think of health as something permanent and final, to be counted on for the rest of our days, is to deny the passage of time and its impact on our fragile physical frames.

# PART TWO
# THREATS TO HOPE

# 12. RELAPSE AND ITS EMOTIONAL FALLOUT

*Any disease introduces a doubleness into life—an "it,"*
*with its own needs, demands, limitations.* [55]

The most infuriating thing about this illness is that little spurts of strength are followed, inevitably, by relapses, when the whole raft of symptoms comes cascading back, like pent-up water bursting through a dike. After weeks of lying down most of the time, measuring my expenditure of energy scrupulously, taking every supplement and medication that had been suggested, padding all activities on each side with hours of rest, a little strength emerged from my depleted body. I had a day or two when head and eye pain were muted, even manageable. Oh, maybe, just maybe, there was hope of progress. Blessed thought! But then, just as quickly, it all came flooding back, like a deformed counter-self dragging behind me like a ball and chain. No matter how hard I tried to relegate it to the sidelines, illness forced itself to the forefront.

Consequently, even in its mild forms, I must monitor the situation hour to hour, sometimes moment to moment. "How are you now?" I ask. "What is possible here?" "What's too much?" "What punishment will you exact if I do this or that?"

In the first year or two, my experiences of relapse were frightening enough to make me flat-out obedient to the beast. If I could regress this far this quickly, maybe one of these times I would be pinned permanently under the cliff. So I adopted the posture of a servant afraid of her abusive master. A smart tactic, I thought. Yet after a while, when I saw that the beast was not going to kill me, I became bolder and allowed myself some rage. Like a bee that had just been recaptured after a brief taste of freedom, my wings beat wildly against the jar's glass walls. I buzzed around the lid repeatedly, to exhaustion, looking for a way out. Ironically, when short spells of steadiness emerged, and the symptoms shifted ever so slightly from foreground to background, I was less willing to accept this as my permanent state. Some innate instinct rose up in me to be my advocate, and a fierce one at that. "NO, I WILL NOT BACK DOWN!" she said to no one in particular. Brief periods of relief spawned a hope that more were possible. A little bit of hope went a long way.

Those bursts of hope notwithstanding, relapses completely flattened me, physically, emotionally, and spiritually. The back-and-forth of slight recovery, followed by relapse had me alternately terrified, combative, subdued, furious, hopeful, depressed, protective, anguished, and stubborn enough to seek help on my own behalf.

This demon, illness, has forced me, time and again, to say who I am—like Odysseus of Greek legend, who had to shout out his name to the Cyclops. And who am I? Many things. A fighter, achiever, seeker, pleader, pray-er, learner, lamenter, appreciator, reacher, hoper, privileged one. Most of all I am Julie, wrestling for a blessing. Like Jacob of biblical lore, sometimes my wrestling has been with God. But in general, I have been wrestling health for a blessing, a subject I will address in chapters to come.

Another fallout from illness is that physical pain makes living in the present difficult. In order to hang on to hope, I either turn to memories of the past, when I was healthy and able to be my full-bodied, free-spirited, athletic self, or I project wistfully into a distant future, with the hope of finding at least some modicum of strength again.

One of the practices common to most religious traditions, including mindfulness meditation in Buddhism, centering prayer in Christianity, and keeping Sabbath in Judaism, is the emphasis on being in the present. I understand the spirit of this teaching. Those of us living in a fast-paced culture, hell-bent on moving out of the present into the future, can abandon the present so completely that we miss out on life in the here and now. Given this fact, being fully alive and attentive in the present can be utterly transforming. It leaves us open and available for sustaining connections with ourselves, with others, with God, and with subtle levels of reality.

The plain truth of the matter, however, is that the genuine desire to be present here and now bites the dust again and again when you are physically in pain. You try to practice receiving in any way you can, and that may not be in the present. It may mean tapping a memory of the past or relying on the imagination to project ahead in time. In illness, a lot of ideals fly out the window and you try to find hope by any means available.

When the flickering of symptoms returns, signaling my body's rebellion, they can sometimes be tamed by a whole regimen of antidotes—a different homeopathic remedy; migraine, sleep, and pain medication; natural hormone replacements; digestive aids; eye drops; etc. If I commit to all these practices, the illness sometimes sheathes its stash of knives. But that is never assured. At times nothing works; my body is simply off-kilter like a capsized boat and there seems no way to right her. I have to abandon all expectation that this particular act will lead to that particular result, that cause and effect is the rule. In fact, on many occasions, when I had confidence that a homeopathic remedy would be of help, it proved too strong or too weak, triggering another flare-up. Or pain medication would not work at all. I was a defeated mountain climber, doubled over in the snow, bracing herself with all she's got against gale force winds.

Simply continuing requires forging a narrow passage between denial at one extreme and overindulgence of the illness on the other. The fact is, disease has a sovereignty about it, with its own particular rules. And one cannot escape its dominion. I think often of Donald Hall's comment about the months he and his wife, Jane, spent in the grueling process of a bone marrow transplant at the Fred Hutchinson Cancer Center in Seattle. During those long days and weeks, the disease covered the entire canvas of their lives. "Our only address," he wrote, "was leukemia."[56]

At times, when the tiger returned with a vengeance, I tried another tack. "Just ride him, honey," I told myself, "like one would ride a bucking bronco." The object in this rodeo was not to subdue the beast, or be naive enough to think I could outlast him. It was more like trying to go with the rhythms of the monster. As in Outward Bound's well-worn motto: "If you can't get out of the predicament, get into it." Yeah, right. Neither physical pain nor fear necessarily responds to coaching.

Odd as it may seem, for years I refused to surrender to the belief that this illness was chronic. It was as if accepting that label was to lower a boom that could never be lifted. It would brand me with an identifying mark congealed around me like a roof and four walls. She's got chronic fatigue, fibromyalgia, and immune dysfunction syndrome. As my family practice doctor said when he heard this diagnosis, "Oh, well, you will never be completely out from under that." He did not mean to be uttering a life sentence, I am sure, but that's how it felt. No wonder I slipped and shimmied out of that bridle every time. In about year eight I had to agree that this illness was chronic, even though I consistently hedged my bets, telling myself that chronic need not imply lifelong. That trust/stubbornness has been central to my hope.

When something inside me insists on hope, hope responds, helping me keep an open view of the future. It declares that all the facts are not yet in. For example, when the physician I just mentioned told me I would never be completely out from under CFIDS, some insistent inward advocate stood up and said, "I will not accept that as the only possible outcome! I just will not." The downside of this attitude is that setbacks have come (not surprisingly) from my constant testing of the limits of this corral. For better and for worse, this is my true nature. I am the tireless terrier scratching at the door, the former athlete trying to walk a little farther today than I did yesterday. Many times a week, I focus my gaze on one line, hurriedly scribbled on a sticky note that is taped at eye level above my computer: "Hope is a dream committed to the discipline of becoming a fact."[57] It's not like a person can achieve health. Health is both a gift and the fruit of lots of reaching.

# 13. OTHER THREATS TO HOPE

*Those who know how close the connection is between the state of mind of a person—his courage and hope, or lack of them—and the state of immunity of his body will understand that the sudden loss of hope and courage can have a deadly effect.*[58]

## BEING WEDDED TO A PARTICULAR TIMETABLE

The trick is to hold fast to your hope yet hold lightly to its timing. How about this for an example: an old Nicaraguan woman was talking with journalists who stood in front of a new school that had just been built in a rural province. When they asked her if she could read, she said with a toothless smile: "Not yet." Hers was a hope that was not time bound.

In *Man's Search for Meaning*, his chronicle of surviving the Nazi prison camp of Auschwitz, Austrian psychiatrist Victor Frankl noted that the death rate among his fellow prisoners spiked precipitously at particular times of the year, especially around holidays like Passover or Christmas. It was not that conditions in the camp had changed significantly during these periods. The food remained horrible; hard labor was as grueling and humiliating as ever. It was simply that many people had pinned their hopes on being released by a particular date, and when that date came and went without any sign of liberation, it was too much to bear. As in the mind and heart, so in the body; with the loss of hope, life drained away, too.

The death rate in the week between Christmas 1944 and New Year's 1945 increased in camp beyond all previous experience . . . the majority of prisoners lived in the naive hope that they would be home again by Christmas. As the time drew nearer and there was no encouraging news, the prisoners lost courage and disappointment overcame them.[59]

# The Absolutizing Instinct

Another threat to hope comes with trying to live ideals that are not human. Its chief example is perfectionism. When I was a seminary student in Princeton, New Jersey, I used to run most every afternoon, with my friends, down along an idyllic road bordering Springdale Golf Club and the grounds of Princeton University's graduate school. It was good exercise, but more than that, being outdoors, in the stunning beauty of that place, helped clear the mind and get me away from the intensity of learning Greek and Hebrew. The spectacular grounds, with their medieval-looking towers and spires, amid the hilly New Jersey countryside, could have been mistaken for Camelot. At the end of each run, we would climb the steep stairway up to the graduate tower, with its spectacular view. Hidden beneath this idyllic setting, however, was a subterranean cancer that could be deadly.

One late spring day, after finals were over, we noticed that the tower stairway was blocked off. It took several inquiries on our part to discover the reason for its closure. Over the course of years, several graduate students had jumped to their deaths from that spire after receiving their final grades, which were not perfect, as they expected them to be. Now I ask you, how could it be that academic grades were—and are—held in such esteem that missing their mark was enough to end the life of a young person, gifted and bright enough to have been accepted at one of our country's most elite institutions? It is possible when perfectionism is present, because perfectionism "holds that anything less than total victory is failure . . . it is a stick with which to beat the possible."[60] This is one of hope's gravest shadows, for "nothing creates as much hopelessness as an ideal that is not human," writes Lynch.[61] Unrealistic ideals make it hard for a person to celebrate ordinary accomplishments.

On a far more ordinary scale, this same nemesis, achievement orientation, is, I think, a force familiar to many of us. It is certainly alive and well in me. It keeps us constantly driving and striving, propelled by a mind-set that makes us feel that neither who we are nor what we do is ever enough if it does not meet a standard of perfection. As the old saying has it:

Good, better, best
Never let it rest,
Till the good is better,
And the better best.

Perfectionism, high ideals, unrealistic expectations, specific timetables— all can be clustered under an umbrella that William Lynch refers to as the "absolutizing instinct." By that he means:

. . . an instinct, and a way of seeing that magnifies. In its presence each thing
loses its true perspective and its true edges. The good becomes the tremendously good, the evil becomes the absolutely evil, the gray becomes the black
or white. . . . The small becomes the big. But above all, everything assumes a
greater weight than it has, and becomes a greater burden . . . it is . . . the creator of idols . . . fantasy, distortion, magnification. . . . In its presence nothing
measures up.[62]

In the face of this instinct, things lose their true perspective. One negative
comment made by a friend leads to the assumption that the person doesn't like
us at all. The fact that we didn't do well on one math test means we are stupid in
every other subject, too. The absolutizing instinct can be seen in the way athletics
in America operates on a winner-take-all mentality. In this worldview, if a team
wins fifteen games but loses only one—the championship—it is a loser, and the
team with a perfect record the only winner.

Even our language can take on an "absolutizing" character. I am thinking
of words like *never* and *always*. Kids can say of their parents: "She never lets me
do such and so." "He always says no on that." Dramatic exaggerations like these
may have a kernel of truth in them, but they are rarely completely true. A child
who says these things has not yet lived into the ability to recognize life's nuances
and to see her current circumstances against a larger background that relativizes
absolutes.

Sometimes, in the depths of illness, my own mind fell into this trap. "Maybe
I will *never* round this corner," I would think. "Maybe I'll *always* be swimming
in this small cage, pinned between total debilitation and a meager amount of
energy. Maybe the best I can hope for is to be let out into the clear sunlight for a
few hours now and then." Hope seemed a distant thing. It shimmered up ahead,
like heat radiating from the pavement, an elusive mirage. Though I reached and
reached for it, it stayed far off.

For some of us, our steepest learning curve has been in the realm of unrealistic expectations; namely that we could and should please everyone, and that we
could and should be liked by everyone. These instincts may need the tempering
of kindness toward one's self.

For others, it's the expectation that we do well in every arena that is the
killer. We think we should always be an attentive spouse or partner, a loving parent, a thoughtful neighbor, a good performer in our work, a contributor to the
greater good, physically fit, faithful to our spiritual practice, a witty and dependable friend, etc., etc., etc. Talk about a set-up for hopelessness! There's nothing
wrong with striving as long as it's accompanied by mercy, but when nothing
measures up and the bar is set high on every count, we are in trouble. When the

absolutizing instinct is in high gear, we are not able "to tolerate the fundamental ambivalences that belong to the heart of the creative world."[63] Life is messy.

## LIVING WITH LIMITS

A person need not suffer illness to come face-to-face with life's limits, and this learning is essential to healthy hope. I distinctly remember a conversation in which a friend and mentor said to me, rather off-handedly: "Well, you know, there are limits to what we can expect from this life." This was not a disparaging remark at all. It was a voice of wisdom. I was in my early twenties then, however, young and still budding, feeling my oats. Life was all about possibilities. Limits? To this life? I chewed on those few words for a bit, but could not swallow them. Was this really so? There was a fifteen-year difference between us, and I had not lived into the truth of her words. I would learn this from experience in due time, but I was not prepared to accept that she was right, in *that* moment. I am quite sure now that what she meant was, "This is human life, honey, not heaven. It is glorious in so many ways, but it's flawed and imperfect as well, and we have to learn to love life as it is."

## THE GO-IT-ALONE, DO-IT-MYSELF INSTINCT

As I have said earlier, one of the cultural trappings in a country with as many resources as ours is the assumption that we can or need to be able to solve problems ourselves. This holds true for us as individuals and as a nation. What a set-up for disappointment and possible shame at ever asking for help. To live as if hope is only a private, interior resource is an impossible burden to place on hope. Hope is integrally related to help. For some of us, the willingness to ask for help, and the surprising gift of receiving it, can bolster hope.

# 14.

# SPIRITUAL FALLOUT: ILLNESS "CAN RUIN YOUR MANNERS TOWARD GOD"[64]

*Therefore I will not restrain my mouth;*
*I will speak in the anguish of my spirit;*
*I will complain in the bitterness of my soul.*
                                        —Job 7:11

## WHEN IT'S DIFFICULT TO PRAY

When the poet Jane Kenyon said of manic depression that it "ruined her manners toward God," she might have been speaking about the effects of any chronic condition. After a while, fatigue settles in from having expended all that energy on sheer coping. The flaring of hope followed by loss of hope can lead to emotional flatness. When you have reached and reached for help, only to find none, anguish and grief might well move in alongside fatigue, too. This simmering stew can dull a person. In my case, I lost all capacity for appreciation. Gratitude and trust seemed like remote qualities with which I used to be familiar, but was now completely estranged from. I felt like a spiritual dud. Prayer took on a listless, weary character. Occasionally I could muster a one word plea: *Help!* or even two words: *Thank you,* but for the most part, hope, and my spiritual life with it, went underground.

Here was the crux of the challenge: it's hard to believe in a personal God whose comfort and healing power are available when your own situation doesn't seem to shift toward healing. Yet you can't cry out to God without being personal. The only way to reconcile the two is to shout at God. I knew what a poor child in New York City named Lucia meant when she said she "knows God's heart is already in the world," but wishes "he would push the heart more into it. Not just halfway. Push it more!"[65] I have wanted to say just this to God myself. "Try harder, God. I know you can do it (heal me). So what's preventing you from doing so?"

Compared to that child, I live replete with privilege. Yet all of us are humbled, at some time or other, by the gaps between that Healing Presence we want to experience and our seeming distance from it. I have learned to pray with as much honesty as possible and to pray if and when I can.

On some days, I had the energy to keep a list in my journal of every generous gesture extended to me that I could remember—from neighbors who brought food to friends who took me to doctor's appointments or shoveled my sidewalk. At other times, I had neither the heart nor the words for prayer.

One summer, lying prone, again, after another devastating relapse, I had the good fortune to look out onto a beautiful ocean landscape. Cedar trees and Douglas fir formed the dark ridge of a neighboring island in the Puget Sound. The sunlight danced with water all afternoon, and I realized that gazing, or appreciative seeing, would have to be my prayer form because it was all I could give. Noticing beauty was the only way I could say to God: "I see your handiwork. Thank you." Sometime later I remembered that I was in good company. In the Eastern Orthodox tradition of Christianity, gazing into the faces of icons and "reading" sacred history by means of pictures has been a prayer form for centuries. That can be enough.

Accepting one's spiritual limits can be a boon to hope. At least it was for me. Piling more demands on myself would have stretched prayer into something too difficult, too disingenuous, and it would break hope's back when it was already struggling. Embracing my limits took me off the hook from trying to do something that felt impossible. Call it kindness toward self. I could not do more than gaze with limp appreciation.

In my experience of meeting people for spiritual direction and leading many retreats, I have learned how frequently people talk about feeling inadequate about their spiritual lives. They should really pray more often than they do or more fervently; if only they could meditate regularly, not just on the fly. If they were truly disciplined, they would carve out space for reflection and journaling on a daily basis. I say those same things, too. And while I can't disagree that there is no substitute for beating a path to *the well* on a regular basis, I think if we were kinder toward ourselves, we might give ourselves permission to pray as we can, not as we cannot, and to know that there are many ways of prayer.

## AS THE BODY GOES, SO GOES HOPE

One of my core learnings in this apprenticeship to hope through illness is this: Whatever our age or station in life, as the body goes, so goes hope. Try as we might to spiritualize it, our emotional and spiritual well-being are intricately bound up with our physical well-being. Being rested and well nourished can make all the difference in a hopeful or a despairing outlook. As Oscar Wilde is reported to have said, "After a good dinner one can forgive almost anybody, even one's own relations." My own spiritual director said to me once, "Honey, you don't need spiritual direction today; you need a nap." And she was right.

When I was in the depth of illness, if someone tried to spiritualize hope, it made me furious. I distinctly remember a day I felt awful but went to a board meeting anyway. Pride having given way to necessity years before, I leaned my head and upper body down on the boardroom table. A woman (health care provider) sat down next to me and inquired about how I was feeling. My body language made the answer obvious. I felt miserable. A few minutes into our conversation she made a comment that lit my fuse. "But of course not all of you has been touched by illness," she proclaimed. "There's a spiritual dimension in each of us that is bigger than the pain." "You wanna bet?" I wanted to say. "How would you know?" And "If that is true, how about if you take me there; I could really use a reprieve right now." How dare she issue a pronouncement about the presence of land when I was sinking beneath the waves right in front of her. The tone of superiority made me wish I had the courage to clobber her for this insensitive platitude. Or to scream: "Look! That's a nice idea on paper, but when excruciating pain is screaming from every system in your body, there is no space that's quiet and free. Pain has soaked through the whole canvas. So don't lay your trip on me."

Even if your physical condition does not change, hope is buoyed when someone listens to you with genuine empathy. It is difficult to describe how all-pervasive an illness can feel to someone who has never experienced it. Those who have not suffered a debilitating illness do not know the power of pain's dominion. "When you are that sick, there is nothing wherever you look that is not sickness."[66]

This woman did not mean to be condescending, and I happen to share her belief that we each harbor within us a sacred center. But illness can distance a person from it, and this was not the moment to proclaim it. You can't simply leap over physical pain to land in a waterproof hope that's on the sidelines, out of the storm. That's not how illness works, and it's not how hope works either! If anything is "spiritual" for the sick person in such times, it is having her pain acknowledged and believed. When another person expresses understanding about how difficult it must be to bear long pain, it's worth so much. Yet, ironically, it is in the presence of kindness that my pain intensifies, allowing me to feel it more deeply. This is the gift—and challenge—of being heard. I have come to think of empathy and kindness as the most precious of qualities, *the* jewels in the human crown.

In Hmong culture, when people are seriously ill for a long time, they believe the spirit leaves the body. I agree. Whether I would call it the soul or not, something did die in me in those long years of illness, something related to the soul. Suffering can rob us of our power and highlight our inabilities. But I also remember vividly the moment and the place where my soul came back. I was leading a retreat in an upstairs room of a former convent, now a retreat center in St. Paul. It was early December. Sunlight filtered in through the windows and the trees were cloaked in a light dusting of snow. I was leading others in a meditation, but it was I who was being carried along. It felt like my body, growing ever stronger, was a trustworthy vessel for the soul again, able to contain her. I had the sensation of my being expanding, and joy, pure joy, welled up.

## THE GOD QUESTIONS

One summer, while I was leading a retreat, a young seminarian who knew of my illness asked whether I believed that God was a healer. While I had lived with that question close-up for many years, I was not fully prepared to answer him in that moment. What I knew was that illness can take us back to an early time in life, where we answered (mostly unconsciously) the question as to whether life was trustworthy or not. If faith is the ongoing process of deciding what is worthy of being at the heart's core, illness calls that question again. And again. And again.

Having given more time to this question, this is what I would say to the seminarian now. I do believe God is a healing force, but neither God nor faith in God exempts us from suffering. Furthermore, if you try to discern the nature of God in the trajectory of just one human life, you may leave out more than you include. You may not find evidence of healing.

We are tiny specks on a planet that is itself a tiny speck, in a universe of trillions of stars, billions of galaxies, and millions of suns. So our worldview, even at its most expansive, is miniscule. It could be compared to the circumference of a straw. There is a tenet in Hinduism that says it takes forty-four million people to offer even a glimpse of God. Even then, our knowing is only an approximation. While our lives can and do manifest the sacred, and while countless people have experienced healing that they attribute to God, you and I may not be cured of an illness we desperately wish would leave, at least not in this lifetime. This is not to say, however, that God does not care about us as individuals, nor that our circumstances do not matter. One way to honor the lingering questions and unanswered riddles is to bring them to God in prayer without censoring them or dressing them up. If honesty is central to hope, it is also central to prayer.

## REFRAMING WHAT IS SACRED

Our culture does not count persistence or perseverance very highly, outside of the realm of sports or business. Yet if there's any gift that can come out of long illness (or any long challenge), maybe it's the staying through, the staying with, the not abandoning one's essential self even when it feels buried under a mountain of suffering. That's what we hope for most in our relationships, after all—that people will stay with us, will stay in the challenge alongside us, will not leave. Perseverance is not glamorous. It's about putting one foot in front of the other. At times, it is about detaching from specific timetables even while holding out hope for better days to come.

The hardest times for me were when I felt there was no purpose to my suffering, that it didn't lead to anything. It wasn't making me a kinder, more empathetic person; it was gnawing away at my better self. The pain could not be converted, like energy, to some other use. Its sole function was to lay me flat. If I had to say where anything good comes out of trial, I hope it is a larger capacity to respond to the pain of others, though I do not know for sure if that is true. Maybe the fighter in me, in all of us, is a sacred force that refuses to die, even when it is wounded.

# 15. FALSE HOPE

*The hope that the Publishers Clearing House sweepstakes will come to you, that the American dream will come true, that electoral politics will reform itself, is hope that paralyzes people's ability to rebel, to reject, to critique, to demand, and to make change. False hope can be a Yes to deprivation, an acquiescence to a lie. Official hope can be the bullying that tells the marginalized to shut up because everything is fine or will be. In its dilute forms, false hope is not so far from despair, for both can be paralyzing.* [67]

Sometimes false hope is neither deceitful nor dangerous, just overconfident or promissory. I'm thinking here of the claims made by advertisers about bran cereal—sure to lower your cholesterol or stave off colon cancer, a promise that can't be proven, though it may sell a lot of cereal. Then there's the kind of false hope that fends off commitment and keeps you waiting, when in fact, a decision has already been made. A parent will say to a child's request, "We'll talk about it later," or "I will think about it," when in fact, she has already made up her mind, and the child knows it, intuitively.

There are silly versions of false hope, chain letters promising money. Or the more pernicious—insurance schemes that bilk money from vulnerable people through completely false promises. What about indulgences, sold by the medieval Roman Catholic Church, in exchange for the assurance your sins would be forgiven and your path to heaven confirmed.

Some versions of fraudulent hope carry devastating consequences. Recall how the Nazis used propaganda to lead certain Jewish communities along in the hope that the latest roundups were truly the last. While there was pervasive horror associated with the true destination of deportation trains, a hope also lingered that the end might not be death, but useful labor. Hadn't postcards arrived from previous deportees to the "family camps" in Auschwitz extolling the merits of the place?

In the summer of 1944, a commission of the International Red Cross came to inspect the ghetto of Terezin (Theresienstadt). Elaborate preparations had been made for this visit, including a propaganda film that portrayed freshly painted buildings, lovely gardens, stores filled with goods, and the apartments of prominent prisoners lavishly decorated with new furniture. Theresienstadt became known as the "Kingdom of Deceit," fraudulent, spurious hope at its most evil. But often false hope is less conspicuous; it is braided through the values a culture takes for granted.

## A Tutorial in Unrealistic Hope

Several years ago, I led an overnight retreat for two dozen high school students from a charter school in a poor, working-class neighborhood in East St. Paul. Many of these kids' parents were in jail, others had died, some suffered from debilitating addictions, a fair number were unemployed, and more than a few spoke no English. Many of these kids were responsible for younger siblings, other relatives, and vulnerable adults.

This school is a true beacon of hope in the community; staff members know they have just one card to play in a deck heavily stacked against these kids. No matter. They will play this one card for all it is worth. While the kids going on retreat were all juniors in high school, many seemed much younger. Most were African American and Hmong; a small handful were white. They were full of energy and anticipation, having never been on a retreat before.

One of our goals was to broach the subject of their future. We were well aware that this was emotionally tricky territory. Few had entertained the question of life beyond high school at all. Almost no one had much support at home for checking out vocational options or finding a job and mapping out a future. In fact, the future must have seemed either completely blank or frightening to them.

In one exercise, we invited each student to make a collage. One side was to depict their current life, the other side their preferred future. There was clear resistance to this project from every corner. I could see it in their faces: "Oh, God, you mean we really haveta do this?" they asked. Despite their hesitancy, the project gathered momentum. But as each one displayed their visual representations of the future, my gut tightened. Almost every young male had a large car depicted in his future—black Mercedes, shiny SUVs with fancy tires, MG convertibles, Cadillacs. Most also had pictures of sprawling luxury homes with three-car garages and beautiful landscaping. Many of the boys had pictures of basketball stars, even though most of them do not own a basketball hoop, nor did their school have a basketball team. The girls' depictions of the future usually included children, along with a nice house. I recall a few fur coats.

It was obvious from the start that these kids were completely at a loss about their future. No one had helped them consider their options. This exercise enabled them to express their hopes, which turned out to be mostly false.

It would have been cruel to leave their thoughts about the future dangling somewhere between the rarified atmosphere of athletic superstardom or affluent suburbia and earning minimum wage at Burger King. Their teacher, social worker, principal, and I tried gently but persistently to coax more out of them by way of practical steps necessary to forge a future. How were they going to get from here to there? Nearly everyone said either "hard work" or "I dunno." Most of them might as well have said "a miracle" or "a benefactor." Were they simply expressing hopelessness? Or were they expressing our culture's message that money and all it can buy is the way to happiness? Here was hope reduced to the big-ticket items writ large on television and trumpeted by advertisers. One could call this a failure of imagination, hope replaced largely by fantasy.

I felt afraid for these kids. They hoped to pluck rarified fruit, available only at the highest branches of the tree. Yet what they needed was a ladder extended to them, with footholds close enough to the ground of current reality to grab on to from here. They needed practical help and tangible skills to move forward.

> The first task of . . . the imagination, if it is to be healing, is to find a way through fantasy. . . . The second task of such an imagination is to create perspectives for the facts it has found.[68]

## Authentic Hope Replaces Unrealistic Hope

The exercise we got right came as a surprise to the kids. Each one received handwritten, personalized letters from their teachers, social worker, principal, and office staff conveying the potential they saw in this student and acknowledging their courage in dealing with their own particular hardships. Like small mirrors, fingered carefully, each letter was read and reread, as if it took more than one reading to believe the message. To know that someone saw their best selves was life-giving, to be sure. One had the gift of kindness, for example; another had a rollicking sense of humor; someone else had a talent for drawing, or a sensitive way of helping younger children. Each letter-writer was at pains to say how much the student was cared about. Watching them read their letters was like watching parched plants revive, almost instantaneously, from an infusion of kindness—one of hope's handmaidens.

# 16. PROVISIONAL HOPE

*Hope is not the same as joy that things are going well, or willingness to invest in enterprises that are obviously heading for success, but rather an ability to work for something because it is good.*[69]

There are many degrees between genuine hope and its stand-in: false, counterfeit, fraudulent, artificial, or chemically induced hope, whose packaging often beguiles. After years of concerted effort, a good friend of mine has made a tremendous breakthrough in her struggle with weight. She has found a way to get that demon to lie down. At times in the past, she got the creature to heel, only to have it break loose again, chasing her around the pen with its horns. Happily, it has been forcibly tethered. She lost nearly seventy pounds and now, three or four years later, is inhabiting her life free of its rampages. Thanks to a strict diet plan and the modeling of people who actually made the radical changes she has hoped for (the most important source of hope, she says), she has dramatically transformed her relationship to food.

She says of the numerous diets she tried—even though none proved to be the one to bring such dramatic results—that all of them were necessary. "People need intermediate hope," she muses, "even if it only helps take them a few steps toward the future they envision. Furthermore," she cautioned, "the term *fraudulent* is a mean word." This is a new thought for me. I suddenly see that even the term *false hope* may be too harsh. Unrealistic hope is a more accurate name.

Our thinking about hope can easily have its own either/or, absolutizing tendencies. Either it is completely pure, bona fide, top-grade hope (hope for peace, for the well-being of our children, and for the health of the planet) or completely bogus (to win the Publishers Clearing House Sweepstakes, to own luxury homes), which leaves out a whole range of necessary hopes, like hopes for belonging and relationship, hopes for success in school or business.

There is a whole range of provisional hopes—some more critical than others. I am thinking here of interim governments and the crucial role they play in countries in which former leaders have been voted out of office, or dethroned unceremoniously, while the new, more permanent government is still being formed.

This concept has emerged in the last century. The most famous example is the one declared in the wake of the abdication of Tsar Nicholas the Second of Russia in the spring of 1917. It was based on the idea that the establishment of a valid government requires consent of the sovereign (which in modern parlance means the people), and it was designed to provide basic government services while the constitutional process of establishing a government was under way.

Suffice it to say these processes are not always successful. If a strong man (or woman) seizes the reins of power and rules as an autocrat, the whole notion of a provisional government goes down the drain. This form of government is tied up with shared understandings of legitimacy and sovereignty.

We depend on certain forms of provisional hope on a day-to-day basis. A spare tire may not be a long-term solution, but it will get you as far as the service station to get the permanent one repaired. Kidney dialysis is not a substitute for a new kidney, but many people cannot have a kidney transplant, and dialysis extends and enhances their lives. Duct tape holds things together, not beautifully, to be sure, but together all the same. Coping may not be thriving, but it beats the alternative. So let's salute provisional hope in whatever form it may come.

# PART THREE
# HOPE'S SIBLINGS:
# TRUTH, FAITH, MEANING

# 17. FINDING MEANING TRUMPS PARTICULAR OUTCOMES

*Just as meaning transcends the relative world whose meaning it constitutes, so faith in meaning transcends all relative utility, and is therefore independent of how things turn out.*[70]

There is a hope that does not have its hands on the controls trying to steer particular outcomes, but a hope "that keeps its hand on the plough no matter how deep the furrow" or how tiny the seeds. Hope, in this case, is a verb. In the end, I believe hope is more closely tied to finding meaning than to specific outcomes. This kind of hope is a dimension of the spirit, an orientation of the heart. "It is not the belief that 'everything will turn out well,' but the certainty that something makes sense, regardless of how it turns out."[71]

I find myself drawing again and again from Vaclav Havel's letters from prison, in which he had to jettison naive hope and hold to something stronger. He said of himself: "I don't share such a belief [that everything will turn out well] and consider it—when expressed in that general way—a dangerous illusion."[72]

This attitude is personified for me by four indomitable Irish nuns in their late seventies and early eighties, who also happen to be biological sisters. The McDonalds—Jane, Bridget, Rita, and Kate—continue to be among the most visible and outspoken advocates for social justice in our community. Among other protests, they and their cohorts have quietly demonstrated, at 6:15 a.m. every Wednesday morning, outside the headquarters of a defense contractor that produces, among other things, cluster bombs. They have done so for over twenty years. When I ask Bridget if she thinks their years of protest have made a dent in anyone's conscience, she responds: "Oh, I don't know, but it's been the right thing to do." Now here is hope with the long view in mind. These folks have not quit demonstrating just because results have been slow in coming and difficult, if not impossible, to measure. Theirs is, rather, a sense that these actions have meaning in themselves.

The primary quality of hope is not certainty, but vision and imagination. Hope is not certain of a particular future, but it can envision it . . . enough to continue, anyway. Optimism lightens our load by promising a good end, even if the basis for the promise is faulty. Hope, by contrast, doesn't lighten the load but strengthens us to carry the load . . . and by claiming that it is all worth it.[73]

The end hope, in the case of these protesters, is the cessation of bomb making. But it is about so much more. It is about finding alternatives to war and finding nonviolent ways to deal with violence. It is about creating a world in which justice prevails.

All of this is to say that each of us must answer the question of what life means, and the answers we find fuel both meaning and hope. Think of it this way: the desire for meaning empowers the search, and finding hope gives us staying power around that which has given us meaning. The search for meaning is what makes us human, what makes us "creators of the 'order of the spirit' . . . capable of stepping beyond ourselves . . . beyond the shadow of our animal foundations."[74]

The key is to hold fast to hope while holding lightly to specific timetables. It is to acknowledge that history moves in epicycles, two steps forward, one step back. Sometimes shifts in attitudes and awareness build slowly, over time, and it's impossible to say just when the tipping point may come.

Americans tend to think in short time spans: hours, days, weeks, maybe years, but not, for the most part, in centuries. Our technologies have brought to us a new unit of time: the nanosecond. Even so, I think we know, down deep, that there are other ways to measure time. References are often made to the practice among some American Indian tribes of making decisions based on their impact on the seventh generation to come. We know this is the right perspective, even if we do not act on it often enough.

Given the fact that living includes constant change, requiring us to face new truths and take in increasingly complex understandings and perspectives, it is an essential life skill to integrate new perspectives into the ways we see and live. Otherwise our worldview is not sufficient to our times. This brings us to the ways we human beings find meaning and come to see our lives within a broader frame.

# 18.

# HOPE SEEKS THE BIGGER PICTURE

*The meaning of any phenomenon lies in its being anchored in something outside itself, and thus in its belonging to some higher or wider context, in its illumination by a more universal perspective; in its being "hung," like a picture, within a higher order.*[75]

## THE ABILITY TO WAIT

One of the attributes of hopeful people is the capacity to see and experience their lives within a larger context. This encompasses a whole bundle of aptitudes. At its most basic, it is about the ability to wait. A three-year-old child begins to realize that "not now" does not mean never. The fact that she cannot have the candy at this moment does not mean she will never be able to have it. I remember what a breakthrough it was when my twin nephews and niece, all about three years old by then, began to use the magic words "next time," a gigantic leap forward in the emotional and intellectual development of children. This new power of thought made all the difference between their erupting into crying spells, even tantrums, when they were disappointed, and learning to trust in a future beyond the present moment. Oh, blessed maturity.

> One of the principle ways in which hope becomes steadier and more mature, less subject to rise and fall . . . is that it develops . . . the capacity "to live contextually." It comes to know that things have contexts and are not absolute, atomic units . . . the more mature the life, the larger is the time range and the scope of a person's ideas and intentions.[76]

In my own case, and for the other one million people estimated to be suffering from CFIDS, there will obviously be no quick exit into robust, dependable health. Still, if we keep the long-term view in mind, there is legitimate cause for hope. Given the number of health care professionals and researchers working on a cure for this disease, it seems likely that someone will eventually trip the switch, crack the code, and find a treatment that will free us from this quagmire of debilitating symptoms. The recent discovery of genetic causes of CFIDS is cause for hope, something I will return to in a later chapter. The more we know about the roots of this illness, the better chance we have of treating it effectively. I realize that this may or may not make the present any less challenging. In the meantime, it's about holding on, widening the lens beyond the present, and leaning into the future with expectation.

## A Broader View

Sometimes the simple act of leaving town for the weekend, or going away on vacation, is enough to enlarge one's perspective and buoy hope. By putting the routine of our days temporarily behind us, it is easier to see what's off balance in our lives, acknowledge what's going well, and ask whether there might be a better way to carry one's burdens. The fifty-thousand-foot view can strengthen hope without denying real difficulties, because when you are inside the frame, running hard around the squirrel cage, it is hard to see the whole picture.

This is what Sabbath was meant to do. This ancient and revolutionary practice is unique to Judaism, though the habit of honoring nature's rhythms by adhering to regular rhythms of renewal had its antecedents in Babylonia and elsewhere. Let's be clear that Sabbath is about far more than an afternoon nap, or finally having a few hours to clean the house. It is about remembering God, our source, and reminding ourselves that we are not God. Sabbath must be long enough to take leave of one's habits and unhook from the demands of the marketplace so that we can reenter life differently.

You have heard of taking some "R & R." Well, let me suggest that Sabbath encompasses a whole string of intentions, all of which begin with the letter *r*, as do the fruits of these intentions. They have to do with rhythms and renewal.

The first of these is *restoring* wholeness by *resting*, physically. We are embodied, after all, and things go so much better when we are not tired. To find rest requires *relinquishing*, however. You have to *relinquish* control, loosen your grip on your schedule, choose not to respond to the phone or the mail or work, and step away from the world's chief idol—money. On the Sabbath a person *remembers* the past week's goodness, *receives* from life's bounty, and *reclaims* one's life as a gift from God. In the process, the ego *returns* to its rightful place (in the back seat). Observing Sabbath *rituals regularly*, not just once in a while, can help a person find perspective and *reestablish* a relationship with life's natural *rhythms*. If a person has had time and space enough to *reimagine* life differently, it really is possible to *reenter* life differently on Sunday or Monday morning. In a crowning tribute to the power of Sabbath, Rabbi

Abraham Joshua Heschel said: "Every seventh day a miracle comes to pass, the *resurrection* of the soul."[77]

Another aspect of being able to live contextually is the patience and attentiveness to look for subtleties beneath the surface of an event or a situation and to stay curious about the many possible ways to "read" it. For example, while our opinions and attitudes about the war in Iraq may differ greatly, many of us across the world and political spectrum have felt considerable anguish about the loss of so many lives. What may get lost is that something happened one month prior to March of 2003 that had never happened before. Former assistant secretary-general of the United Nations and peace activist Robert Muller spoke of the marches for peace this way:

> Never before in the history of the world has there ever been a global, visible, public, viable, open dialogue and conversation about the very legitimacy of war. . . . The millions marching . . . represented something that is not yet fully realized, an extraordinary potential . . . waiting for some catalyst to bring it into full flower. A new imagination of politics and change may already be seeded here.[78]

## THE ART OF REFRAMING

One way the ability to live contextually takes on flesh and blood is when a person puts into practice one of the most helpful of all life skills—the ability to reframe a situation, to find perspective. Here is what I mean.

Bill Dehn, a friend of my family, was, at six feet eight or nine inches tall, a commanding presence; his children called him "Gov" (for governor). At age seventy-six, he won the national sailboard championship in the over seventy-five category on the Columbia River in Oregon. Not long thereafter, an unexplained numbness in his hand and arm came on. Eventually, when his doctors could offer no answers, he sought help at the Mayo Clinic, where he was diagnosed with ALS (Lou Gehrig's disease). Amyotrophic lateral sclerosis is a devastating illness that causes progressive paralysis. Soon after receiving the news, Bill said to me: "I am a fortunate man. I have had a good life, a privileged life. Of course I would like to live longer, though if I do not, maybe I can at least get into some clinical trials, which could benefit men who come after me."

Twenty years earlier he had participated in clinical trials involving new, cutting-edge treatments for prostate cancer. He founded a support group in Southern California for men with this disease, and this work took him to the nation's capital, where he testified before Congress in support of medical research dollars for prostate cancer. Here, in Bill's response to a virtual death sentence, was the capacity to see his life and death in terms that acknowledged grief and loss, yet experienced that loss within a larger frame.

The late Audre Lorde, poet, essayist, and activist, has a parallel story. During the years she battled advanced liver cancer, she kept a journal, which was published as a book entitled *A Burst of Light*. In the passage to follow, Lorde is writing from a cancer clinic in Berlin during very difficult days. She was trying to balance medical information with her own intuitive wisdom about how to proceed, carefully weighing her treatment options. Part of her work involved her attitudes and outlook.

> How do I hold faith with sun in a sunless place? It is so hard not to counter this despair with a refusal to see. But I have to stay open and filtering no matter what's coming at me, because that arms me in a particularly Black woman's way. When I'm open, I'm also less despairing. . . . I know I can broaden the definition of winning to the point where I can't lose.[79]

What is her burst of light? The hope of avoiding death? No, that would be hope for the wrong thing. "We all have to die at least once," she writes. "Making that death useful would be winning for me."[80] How could it be useful? "By learning not to crumple before . . . uncertainties . . . and by resolving to 'print' [herself] upon the texture of each day *fully* rather than *forever*" (emphasis added).[81]

## HOLDING THE TENSIONS

The ability to embrace paradox is at the heart of contextualizing. It has to do with appreciating life's beauty, given its fragility. "So teach us to count our days that we may gain a wise heart," wrote the psalmist. We are "like a dream, like grass that is renewed in the morning; in the morning it flourishes and is renewed; in the evening it fades and withers" (Psalm 90:5-6, 12). This is not nihilism nor gloom, but staying awake to a reality we prefer to keep veiled: we are mortal beings who will die.

Poet Jane Kenyon writes poignantly about savoring life's ordinary pleasures in the face of death. When her husband, Poet Laureate Donald Hall, was diagnosed with cancer a dozen years or so ago, she wrote the poem "Otherwise." Ironically, Donald Hall is still vibrant in his early eighties, while Jane died of leukemia at age forty-seven.

## Otherwise

I got out of bed
on two strong legs
It might have been
otherwise. I ate
cereal, sweet
milk, ripe, flawless
peach. It might
have been otherwise.
I took the dog uphill
to the birch wood.

At noon I lay down
With my mate. It might
Have been otherwise.
We ate dinner together
At a table with silver
Candlesticks. It might
Have been otherwise.
I slept in a bed
In a room with paintings
On the walls, and
Planned another day
Just like this day.
But one day, I know,
It will be otherwise.[82]

## HAVEL'S HORIZON

One of our wisest thinkers about the capacity to live contextually is Vaclav Havel. In my years as a student of hope, I have returned again and again to his thoughts more than to any other's. Prison formed a bleak backdrop from which he considered life's meaning. And yet, harrowing as it was to be confined, the door slammed shut on freedom, his access to the outer world cut off, it was a refiner's fire, stripping him down to his essence.

Havel returned again and again, in his mind's eye, to the image of a horizon, "the outer rim of the discernible, intelligible or imaginable world," as a source of meaning, and thus of hope. He calls the horizon his *domov* or "home." *Domov*, in Czech, expresses a notion that is close to what English speakers mean by "a sense of belonging."[83] This image/idea did not come to him first when he was a middle-aged man; it arose quite early in his life.

> Ever since childhood, I have felt that I would not be myself—a human being—if I did not live in a permanent and manifold tension with this "horizon" of mine, the source of meaning and hope, and ever since my youth, I've never been certain whether this is an "experience of God" or not. . . . Whatever it is—a horizon without which nothing would have meaning and without which I would not in fact exist— . . . this "intimate, universal" partner of mine . . . is sometimes my conscience, sometimes my hope, sometimes my freedom and sometimes the mystery of the world."[84]

His wife, Olga, became the intense focus of his preoccupations. She was at the heart of his quest for meaning, her love a stabilizing force. His weekly letters to her gave expression to a larger, ongoing dialogue with life itself, an interaction that sustained his heart and mind.

> It's true that you won't find many heartfelt, personal passages specifically addressed to my wife in my prison letters. Even so, I think that Olga is their main hero. . . . That was why I put her name in the title of the book. Doesn't that endless search for a firm point, for certainty, for an absolute horizon that fills those letters say something, in itself, to confirm that?[85]

A loved one can be one's primary reference point, the center of one's horizon. God can be that center—or circumference—too. For some it's their life's work that frames their world. In any case, we human beings need ways to structure our existence, to see in it some purpose.

Just as Audre Lorde tried to make her death useful, one of the ways Havel endured prison, and kept from being completely stymied by his confines, was by deciding to make his prison time useful. He used prison as a means for "reconstitution."

> I truly feel that when I'm cut off from my former commitments for so long, I might somehow achieve inner freedom and a new mastery over myself. I don't intend to revise my view of the world, of course, but rather to find a better way of fulfilling the demands that the world—as I see it—places on me. I don't want to change myself, but to be myself in a better way. . . . I'd like to return at the age of forty-eight not as an irascible old man . . . but rather as the cheerful fellow I once was.[86]

Some degree of freedom was to be found when he recognized an opportunity to consciously exercise choice. This came in the simple ritual of making tea. That small dimension of his time was his own, and the ways he prepared and drank it strengthened his sense of agency, which in turn buoyed hope. He says to Olga:

> I am trying to bring a certain order into my outer life in the form of a deliberate program of "self care," aimed at promoting physical health and steadiness of nerve. Today I'm going to continue that theme with a short essay on tea. When I was outside, I didn't understand the cult of tea that exists in prison, but I wasn't here long before grasping its significance.[87]

Tea becomes a material symbol of freedom:

> It is in effect the only fare that one can prepare oneself, and thus freely: when and how I make it is entirely up to me . . . sitting down to a cup of tea here is a substitute for the world of bars, wine rooms, parties, binges, social life in other words again, something you choose yourself. . . . And in which you realize your freedom in social terms. . . . I look forward to it, and consuming it (which I schedule carefully, so it does not become a formless and random activity) is an extremely important component in my daily "self-care" program.[88]

Hope, in this instance, is not overcome by the difficulty of the present, thanks to the power of choice and the exercising of intention.

## THE CONTEXT OF CONTEXTS

If we were to stay with Havel's image of a horizon as the outermost boundary of knowable reality, we could say that the discoveries of science in the last few decades have radically transformed our knowledge of the universe, in which our own planet courses. This is the context of contexts. The size and dimensions of the universe are staggering. Even "the distance between stars is so vast that there is no way to get a probe to the nearest one in under fifty thousand years with today's best rockets."[89] We know that our human species is the fruit of a fourteen-billion-year unfolding (give or take a billion), and that our being here is the result of "an ever-lengthening list of characteristics that had to be just the way they were for intelligent life to have evolved."[90] We are, if you will excuse the pun, light-years beyond the medieval worldview, which pictured the world in three dimensions— heaven, earth, and underworld.

Whether you or I can comprehend these cosmological discoveries, and whether you and I are even interested in them, each of us must face the question, what happens on the other side of death? Does the end of this life spell the end of hope? Or does it simply represent the limits of our understanding? My own view must be obvious by now; I would say the latter. Still, life beyond this one remains a mystery. In order to speak about our hopes and intuitions about the great beyond, we borrow images of earthly delight—a garden paradise, an overflowing banquet, a realm of justice and peace, a shining city, a new world order where weeping has ended, those who are poor are satisfied, and we reside in the healing embrace of the Beloved of the soul. The term we use to describe the best possible outcome after death is, of course, *heaven*.

Given our modern sensibilities, some might find the concept of heaven naive, or even rather boring. Even so, a public radio station recently noted that 80 percent of Americans believe in heaven, and that percentage increases with people's age. (At which time it is no longer an exercise in speculation.) The dream of heaven is about the fulfillment of longings that will never be fully satisfied in this life. It is the hope beyond all other hopes, the epitome of seeing this life within a larger context. To borrow words from Emily Dickinson that are sometimes used at funerals:

This World is not Conclusion.
A Species stands beyond—
Invisible, as Music—
But positive, as Sound—
It beckons, and it baffles—
Philosophy—don't know—
And though a Riddle, at the last—
Sagacity, must go.[91]

Dickinson is speaking of faith, in the broadest sense of the word. This brings us to the relationship between hope and faith.

# 19.

# Hope's Relationship to Faith

*If faith puts us on the road, hope keeps us there.*[92]

Two things keep most of us going. The first is faith that life has meaning and purpose. The second is hope, the staying power to keep following our sense of meaning and purpose. Faith and hope comprise the architecture of self as surely as beams support a house. They have tremendous impact on each other.

> It's enough for us to feel that just as Being has its own secret order . . . that . . . our lives . . . have a direction, are "known about, valued and ascribed a significance somewhere, and are not—from the cosmic point of view— forgotten. . . . What else is such a feeling—such a hope, such a faith—but a kind of 'petition' to the absolute horizon . . . guaranteeing that nothing ultimately vanishes and . . . therefore nothing is ultimately pointless."[93]

Can a person have hope without faith? Yes, if by faith we mean specifically religious faith. Many people seem to live quite happily without it. However, if by faith we mean trust in the ultimate character of reality, then no. Some might argue this point with me, but I believe it is difficult to find hope if we have no confidence that life has meaning, if all seems haphazard and directionless, our own lives lacking purpose. That has been my experience, anyway.

If I asked you what associations come to mind when you hear the word *faith*, chances are you would say it has to do with religion. You might go on to distinguish between being religious and being spiritual if you have had negative experiences with religion or if there was an assumption that you had to believe certain things in order to have faith.

# A FAITH STANCE THAT CAN LEAD TO LOSS OF HOPE

It is only recently, and primarily in Christianity, that faith has been equated with belief. The consequence of this is that if you believe certain things, like the resurrection of Christ, for example, you have faith. Conversely, if you do not believe this, you do not have faith. This places an impossible burden on faith and makes it a static and primarily creedal stance that is not willing to doubt itself.

My grandmother grew up in this school of thought, and it troubled her greatly that she had doubts about what happens after death. Still mentally sharp and quick-witted at ninety-six, she grew more and more anxious and worried about her level of faith. A God-fearing person who knew herself by the truths of the Bible, she would often say to me, "I wish I had more faith," as if it were something she could fortify by clenching her muscles. No doubt she was influenced by the American "can-do" spirit, which gets us believing that all things are possible if only we try hard enough and believe strongly enough. So when the desired outcome does not come to be, despite our earnest efforts, we may fall into disillusionment, even despair. What I think my grandmother meant was, if only she had enough faith, she would have no fear of dying. Again, what a burden to place on faith! It led to loss of hope, not only in God, but also in the strength of her own lifetime of faith.

I tried to suggest that faith was more a gift than an accomplishment, that it does not necessarily erase all doubt or fear, any more than hope erases all doubt and fear. They are not static virtues. Like the human heart, the valves of its chambers filling with blood, then contracting to force blood through the body, faith too has its rhythms. I have heard it said that one of the primary associations ascribed to God in Judaic tradition is "a grounding pulse." This understanding is worlds away from seeing God as the unmoved mover, or the still point in a changing world. Seeing faith as a gift is also far more permission-giving in regard to the inevitable peaks and valleys in human faith.

A brief look at the origins of the term *faith* frees it from definitions that do not do justice to its vastness. As you will notice in these definitions, faith may include beliefs, but it encompasses so much more.

# FAITH'S ROOTS IN LANGUAGE

The Greek term for faith, *pistis*, is actually closer to our word *trust*, implying that it is more than an intellectual conviction. In Hindu literature, the term equivalent to the English *faith* is *sraddha*. It is "a compound of two words, *srad* (or *strat*), heart, and *dha*, to put. Sraddha means placing one's heart on."[94] Faith is "the ongoing composing of the heart's true resting place; of determining what is worthy to be at the heart's core."[95] In Pali, the language of the original Buddhist texts, the word for faith or trust is similar to the Hindu rendering; *saddha* means "to place the heart upon." In Hebrew, its equivalent, *emunah*, has two distinct associations. One is a literal column or pillar—something reliable enough to lean against—and the other is a "true line." The Latin term *confide* implies that we confide our vulnerabilities and truths only to someone we trust. In Islam, *imam* has to do with truth, as opposed to falsehood. One aspect of *imam* is belief, but it also includes participation in all aspects of religion at a deep level, including the practices of prayer, fasting, pilgrimage, and almsgiving. In a sign of its inclusivity, the Qur'an does not limit the term *mu'min*, or faithful one, to those who follow Islam; it includes whosoever has faith in God.

## BROADENING OUR UNDERSTANDING OF FAITH

What these definitions suggest is that faith, like hope, is a living, pulsing reality. At times it bursts into fullness; at other times it ebbs. Some days we are given to faith; some days we are not. About five days a week I have hope for the world; on the other two I do not. This understanding enables us to see faith and hope, not as ideals that must be rigidly clung to, but as human virtues that pulsate like the air coursing through our lungs. The expectation that they stay in a steady state is not true to life. Yet many of us were taught that you either had faith and hope or you didn't. And if you didn't, heaven help you. Something was wrong with you.

Faith is a verb. It is something we do, not something we have, like a material possession. While religious faith has unique power in its adherents, faith itself is not unique to religious people. We are all involved in the work of composing meaning, whether within a religious tradition or outside its bounds. My mentor and friend, the noted faith development scholar Sharon Parks, says: "To be human is to dwell in faith, to dwell in the sense one makes out of life—what seems ultimately true and dependable about self, world, and cosmos."[96]

Faith is a relationship with a center of power and value that some call God. Faith encompasses many levels of knowing—cognitive, intuitive, affective—and a bedrock trust in the ultimate character of reality.

## FAITH INEVITABLY COLLIDES
## WITH UNINVITED CIRCUMSTANCE

Sooner or later, in almost every life, one's basic sense of trust and hope in life's goodness and fairness is violently shattered by some uninvited circumstance. Whether it be the loss of a loved one, the withering of a career, a serious illness or injury, betrayal, a poor choice, or even a simple disappointment, something happens that threatens one's sense of meaning and hope entirely. In such times, the grand organizing story(ies) by which one navigated and made sense of the world becomes useless, hopelessly out of date. The central realities one used to believe in erode, leaving him or her face-to-face with that terse four-letter word *fate*, which translated can mean: "Uh-oh, I'm done for."

## HOPE AND UNCERTAINTY

The shifting of tectonic plates created by significant loss or change can create a wake of bewilderment, confusion, and loss of hope. It forces a reconfiguring of one's worldview.

In his reflections on the challenge of transition, William Bridges refers to those little wooden Russian doll sets in which each doll has another doll nested inside it. This, he suggests, is an apt symbol for the succession of worlds we move through across the span of a life.

When all is said and done, this process can be a good thing, a healthy thing, even if uncomfortable. I trust people who are willing to acknowledge being baffled more than I do those who seem to harbor few doubts and would not admit to being confused. Why? Because doubting, questioning, and not knowing are part and parcel of hope and faith. For hope to be hope, and not magical thinking or illusion, it must have its eyes wide open to life-as-it-is.

In my own case, illness stripped away the hopes that were actually illusion about my body's invincibility, longevity, and dependable health. Even though both of my grandmothers lived into their late nineties, what I know now, on a cellular level, is that what one takes to be reality can vanish abruptly, in the blink of an eye. When mortality climbed up the steps and took a seat in my living room, there was no avoiding it.

In the new reality that was chronic illness, I reached, instinctively, for tools that would help me dwell in this place. Stories were one of those tools. Narratives serve a primary function in telling us who we are, how we are related to others, and what our purpose is in this realm. They are central to hope and the cornerstones of meaning-making.

In order to be mature in faith, a person must integrate new experiences and awareness. I am thinking particularly about those circumstances that challenge our faith in life's goodness. People who come for spiritual companioning sometimes say to me: "I think I am losing my faith." I take this experience seriously because I know how unnerving it is to feel this way. However, if I listen long enough, it generally seems more accurate to say that the person's faith is not lost, but changing. Due to some new life experience, or challenging truth, they have to broaden their worldview, update their map, and let go of images, metaphors, and understandings of God and life that are no longer adequate. (Not that any metaphors for God are ever adequate.)

In such seasons, hope can help sustain faith by going deeper than a surface-level reading of things.

> Hope keeps faith from identifying the hiddenness of God as absence. When that error is avoided, hope is ready to take the next step—for ourselves and for others who think the world has forgotten them.[97]

I am suggesting that in the times we do not feel particularly hopeful or faithful we might remind ourselves that they are life stances we commit to more than they are steady emotional states.

Many of us can relate to the experience of having hope or faith drain away, not in one fell swoop necessarily, but incrementally, in the face of the too-muchness or too-longness of something. The too-longness of an elderly parent's illness. The too-muchness of a child's destructive behavior. While such struggle can embitter us, it can also soften us, kneading understanding and compassion into the way we see others, ultimately strengthening hope in the process. Poet Mark Doty says of this:

> I can imagine now, where I couldn't before, this long erosion of faith, this steady drawing from one's strength, until what's left is tenuous, transparent. I used to think depression wrong—a failure to see, a rejection of the gifts of one's life, an injustice to the world's bright possibilities. But I understand now, better than I did before.[98]

Maybe you could write the book on what happened to God when you got married. Or how divorce shattered the way you saw your life. Others could say what happens to God with the experience of losing a job, having a baby, traveling to a third-world country, seeing the inside of a prison, taking a big financial risk, staring at a picture of the earth from the moon, visiting the Grand Canyon, being diagnosed with cancer, waking up to racism, experiencing healing, losing a parent. While God may not have changed, a person's perceptions of God certainly can, and do.

This is not to judge bright faith, with its blaze of exuberance, idealism, and possibility. This kind of faith, like young love, is to be celebrated. As the years go on, however, it needs to develop the means to examine and reflect, known in Buddhist teaching as "verifying faith." Without this capacity, the person remains stuck in childhood faith, or in a belief system that hardens into brittle, unthinking, unquestioning faith, unable to integrate new life experiences into the canopy of meaning. Science prides itself on the necessity of revision. Religion ought to have pride in that process, too. When it does not evolve and deepen, religious faith is diminished, content to swim around in the shallows, hugging familiar spaces, afraid to go out in the depths.

> A worthy faith must bear the test of lived experience in the world—our discoveries and disappointments, expectations and betrayals, assumptions and surprises. It is in the ongoing dialogue between self and world, between community and lived reality, that meaning—a faith—takes form.[99]

We must attend to the fresh and present livingness of God, and that requires holding very lightly to our conceptions of the divine. For the more truth we have, the more we know of God.

Even those with mature faith and hope experience bewilderment. It is a companion in the spiritual life. In my experience, more and more seems bound by the category of mystery, so I feel more at home these days with people who say, "The older I get, the less I know," than with those who seem unwavering in their certainty.

Chronic illness purged me of some of my own bedrock hopes and beliefs, particularly a belief in the power of the medical resources of our time, and, secondarily, that the resources of faith could be brought to bear on an emotional and physical crisis. I am one of the fortunate who seems to be moving toward steadier health, and I would say God is present in all the factors contributing to my health, but there is no easy quid-pro-quo equation between faith and healing. There have been many days in which the answer to my pleas for healing could, seemingly, be summed up in one word: silence. No one is exempt from life's cruelties, regardless of their spiritual or religious life.

# 20. HOPE AND TRUTH SIT SIDE BY SIDE

*The first duty of hope is to face the facts directly. If this does not happen, the facts are dealt with indirectly, and they break out underground. "The imagination must be a coping, not an evading instrument."*[100]

Whether we are talking about private, personal hopes or the more public and collective hopes of a community, the starting place in a search for hope is honesty about the truth of things in the present. Several decades ago, journalist Bill Moyers interviewed writer Robert Penn Warren and asked how we could resolve the terrible crises of the day such as decaying cities, unaffordable health care, and poverty. Mr. Warren leaned forward and said, "Well, Bill, for a beginning, I think it would be good if we would stop lying to one another."[101]

Whether we are talking global climate change caused by greenhouse gases, millions of people without health insurance, or the gap between those who are rich and those who are poor, too much is at stake to be satisfied with sugarcoating our most daunting problems, accepting quick fixes, and calling surface-level good news good enough. The longer we do such things, the less available we are to authentic hope. And if we buy into the notion that happiness is mostly about material abundance, we will be in for further loss of hope. We must give birth to consciousness and ways of living that have never been before. This need for transformation will require a tremendous price, especially from those of us who live with privilege.

What language can we draw from in order to open hearts and minds to this need and not close them? We can learn from the biblical prophets' thundering truth-telling several thousand years ago.

## LEARNING FROM THE PROPHETS

Whether we refer to Isaiah or Jeremiah, Amos or Micah, or any of the other prophets in biblical history, each had an overpowering sense of indignation at the way the powers of their day conspired to deceive people, offering versions of reality that were fundamentally false. The prophet's task was to shatter people's complacency. To do that, he or she (yes, there were women prophets) turned to exaggerated language and crackling metaphors that cut like a whip to the bone, exposing realities that *should not have been so*. The Hebrew root of the word *prophet, navar*, means "to bark," and the prophets certainly barked about endangered truth and against idolatry in particular.

Jeremiah drew a parallel between his people's lusts and those of "a restive young camel . . . in her heat sniffing the wind" (Jeremiah 2:23-24). Listen to this curt summation of his people's moral state, by the prophet Isaiah: "We have made a covenant with death, and with Sheol [Hell] we have an agreement; . . . we have made lies our refuge, and in falsehood we have taken shelter" (Isaiah 28:15). "Therefore justice is far from us. . . . Truth stumbles in the public square, and uprightness cannot enter" (Isaiah 59:9, 14).

Can you imagine a modern-day politician going as far as the prophets did in calling people to task for the evil unleashed by corrupt systems? Probably not. We don't tend to vote prophets into office. Their kind of honesty can feel threatening and dangerous. It would not win votes because it would expose realities that would require profound change.

The prophets' ire was often directed at "royal definitions of reality." They saved their most toxic venom for those leaders who counted on the patronage of God, reviling what the biblical scholar calls the inflated, "imperial claims of the empire."[102] The prophet's unenviable task was to offer an alternative view of reality, a job that was never sought and unanimously resisted. No one wanted the role.

Had they only railed against wrongdoing, they would likely have been run off a cliff. In fact, their extraordinary vision and heart-piercing scenarios of what should be, could be, would be—God willing—are some of the most riveting and hopeful passages in all of the Bible. The source of their hope is God and God's sovereignty, which will ultimately win out. In that time:

Justice will dwell in the wilderness,
and righteousness abide in the fruitful field.
The effect of righteousness will be peace,
and the result of righteousness, quietness and trust forever. (Isaiah 32:16-17)

Imagine how this foretelling might have been heard by an anguished people in the barrenness of exile.

For you shall go out in joy,
and be led forth in peace;
the mountains and the hills before you
shall burst into song,
and all the trees of the field shall clap their hands.
Instead of the thorn shall come up the cypress;
instead of the brier shall come up the myrtle;
and it shall be to the LORD for a memorial,
for an everlasting sign that shall not be cut off. (Isaiah 55:12-13)

Isaiah's calling was to offer compelling, poetic scenarios of reality that lay outside the control of the empire. In the face of these compelling alternatives, the official perspectives of "the ruling power lost their absoluteness and their authority because the language of the prophets served to subvert it."[103]

The prophets pleaded with their listeners not to accept the way things were, politically speaking. They appealed to the actions of God that were discontinuous with the past, and pointed to a different future that was not obvious on the surface. "I am about to do a new thing; now it springs forth, do you not perceive it? I will make a way in the wilderness and rivers in the desert" (Isaiah 43:19).

In a contemporary version of risky truth-telling, writer, naturalist, and environmental activist Terry Tempest Williams gave the commencement address to the graduating class of 2003 at the University of Utah. Her niece, Callie Tempest Jones, was among the graduates, which meant that a great many other family members and close friends were in the audience that day. On this score, she shared with the biblical prophets the difficult call to speak costly truths from within her community, a much riskier endeavor than playing it safe when close to home and saving more controversial comments for settings in which she was a visitor and could leave immediately after the address. She wrote:

Unlike most places, where I could simply speak and leave, here I would have to speak and stay, continue living and working within my own state of Utah. I wanted to address my community honestly at this moment in time when a war [the war in Iraq] was dividing so many of us.[104]

She challenged people to risk a lovers' quarrel with their country, challenged them not to wring their hands, but to become active citizens, working to keep democracy alive. She compared closed societies that inspire terror and the tyranny of belief with the open spaces of democracy, in which honest questions can be raised, and disagreement and controversy can be addressed head-on through dialogue. Her closing remarks in that commencement address sounded a plaintive note:

We are no longer citizens. We are media engineered clones wondering who we are and why we feel alone. . . . When democracy disappears, we are asked to accept the way things are. I beg you, as graduates of this distinguished university, do not accept the way things are.[105]

The source of hope here is in a person's willingness to speak the truth about things that should not be so. Truth is hope's handmaiden in that it acknowledges how things really are in the present. Daunting as it is to risk disfavor by challenging the status quo, especially in a time when fears loom large, hope is not served by lies or untruths. Nor can we birth the new if we spend our energy defending present circumstances as if they were the best we could hope for. So we end where we began, in the necessity of truth-telling in the search for hope.

## Do These Distinctions Matter?

Does it really matter whether or not we distinguish faith from hope, or is this just a matter of semantics? The distinctions are important. They help us better understand and honor the powers of hope and faith in our lives. Both are, in part, fruits of the imagination. Both are gifts that have to be nurtured and practiced. In the healthiest scenarios, both hope and faith mature in ways that are ever wiser and ever more adequate.

Hope is the willingness not to give up precisely when we draw no consolation from faith. It doesn't try to determine how God's ways will be shown, but remains open to new and astonishing manifestations of the divine presence. Hope is the retrieval of possibilities that come as gift.[106]

Faith is the ongoing process of composing meaning in the present. Hope is about a way into the future. Faith is the way we "shape into one" the disparate dimensions of life, gathering in the entire spectrum of joys, gladness, sorrows, tragedies, conundrums, and perplexities. Hope is finding a way into the future, grounded in a sense of meaning and purpose. They are inseparable companions, essential elements of our being.

# 21. WHEN HOPE TAKES WORK

*Escalating pain can flood the brain with the kind of visceral input that solidifies hopelessness. This is a vicious cycle. When we feel pain from our physical debility, that pain amplifies our sense of hopelessness; the less hopeful we feel, the fewer endorphins and enkaphalins and more CCK we release. To break that cycle is key. It can be broken by the first sparks of hope: Hope sets off a chain reaction. Hope tempers pain.*[107]

Religious traditions have names for an emotional state of being familiar to most of us. Whether we call it impasse, stuckness, or standstill, it is an uncomfortable place to be. In Roman Catholic teaching, limbo is the abode of souls who had not been admitted to heaven but were not condemned to hell either. Similarly, in Tibetan Buddhism, *bardo* is the name given to a gap between being either dead or alive. Being in such zones is like being forced to idle in what seems like an endless vestibule, unable to move forward toward one's destination.

Some cultures even have dances that ritualize this. There is a dance called the limbo that originated from the West Indies. My parents and their friends used to dance the limbo at parties when they were young. In this dance, the dancer bends backward from the waist and moves with a shuffling step under a horizontal bar that is lowered with each successive pass. If the high jump in a track meet is about height, the limbo is about how low you can go. This most unnatural posture is, needless to say, terribly hard on the back, which cannot maintain this pose for long. Yet as a way to give physical expression to an emotional and spiritual state, it's perfect. Once you have leaned back that far, you are going to have to right yourself again, a motion as difficult as bending backward in the first place.

About five or six years into illness, I had a new appreciation for this subject. I felt deadlocked, not in as rough a shape as I had been earlier, but a long way from any sense of a possible turnaround in health. "There are things you cannot reach," writes Mary Oliver, "but you can reach toward them."[108] I reached and reached, but no help came.

Somehow I needed to find a different internal posture for reaching when it didn't seem that health would arrive anytime soon. I learned how critical it was, in impasse, not to abandon myself. This is torturous learning when physical pain persists, year after year after year. I did not want to be attached to my suffering; I did not want it to so dominate the landscape that nothing else was visible. But pain shoots holes in noble intentions as surely as an archer can decimate a flimsy sheet of plastic with a bull's-eye tacked to a bale of hay. Illness just would not move on.

Enduring limbo may be particularly difficult for achievement-oriented people. Ours is such an activist society that impasse may be rendered unacceptable. We just want to do something, anything, to break the logjam. But when hope goes unrealized, a person has to be honest about his or her feelings—whether cranky, discouraged, weary, or distraught—stick up for him- or herself, and draw on every possible resource, within and without.

## When Hope Takes Work

At some point you might have to get up, strike out in a different direction, and try something new in an attempt to go to bat for yourself. This is what desperation can do.

Sometimes hope takes work. I said earlier that I had a bone to pick with Emily Dickinson. Contrary to her sense that hope had never asked a crumb of her, I have found hoping to be very hard work. After months of resignation and impasse, I knew I could not lie there passively forever.

On the advice of my piano teacher, who grew up in Singapore and was familiar with several Asian healing practices, I did something I would not ordinarily have done. I took my place among a long line of ill people seated on folding chairs in a Vietnamese grocery store in South Minneapolis, parked between a refrigerator full of pigs' feet and shelves lined with a hundred varieties of noodles. Our inelegant postures said it all. A few pressed their arms into their midsections, doubled over in pain. Others hunched forward, heads in their hands. I leaned back against the horizontal ledge of a shelf to rest, while shooting pain in my head and eyes pounded unabated. What a sorry sight we were. No one had energy enough to talk to one another. We simply waited our turn in this makeshift "waiting room," while customers wheeled their carts around the aisles. There were no magazines to peruse or television shows to watch as a means of distraction. We had to be with the reality of our illnesses.

When my turn finally came, the healer, a Vietnamese man I guessed to be in his early sixties, wordlessly motioned me to come forward. I walked up to the desk, jammed in between the wall and a long counter, and sat down in the chair face-to-face with this stranger. He spoke no English, which made me glad that we could skip over the niceties and get right to work on alleviating my pain. First he placed his hands on my wrist to measure my pulse, then asked me to open my mouth wide. After a look at my irises and few brief questions that I did not quite understand, he handed a list of instructions to his assistant behind the counter.

She tore a wide swath of butcher paper from the roll on the wall and divided it into three ample sections. On each piece of paper, she began to build an exotic pile of substances that I could not decipher. Some looked clearly like feathers. Then there were seed pods, taken from large glass jars. A handful of fish skins. On top of that she added dried leaves, fruit rinds, small twigs, and what looked like snake skins. She sprinkled the little mountain of concoctions with twigs and a yellowish pollen (Vietnamese cinnamon?), adding a sprig of an unknown herb and a handful of nuts, duplicating this three times. Each mound looked like something taken from the compost pile or the bottom of a polluted lake. Then she deftly gathered each bundle, securing it at the top with red string, and I walked out the door $54 poorer, with instructions to boil a pile and drink one cup of it twice a day for a week. This was something I earnestly attempted. Truly I did, not once, but twice, though I had to hold my nose and stifle my gagging reflex even to look at the pile. The mysterious brown, watery soup smelled hideous—like a ghastly, putrid swamp. It was downright vile. I could not bear even the smell of this remedy, let alone swallow a cup of it. It sat on the top of my refrigerator for many months until I had shown it to many of my disbelieving friends. It was so gross that one day I unceremoniously threw it out.

While the tea did nothing for my illness, feeling some measure of agency by trying something new was a whole lot better than feeling like a victim. And I sensed that the willingness to be an advocate for myself registered somewhere in my body/soul. A quiet inner voice said: "Thank you for trying. Thank you for 'putting legs' on the desire for healing." Going down the rabbit hole certainly trumps defeat.

# PART FOUR
# AIDS TO HOPE—
# SOURCES OF HOPE

# 22. DETECTING PATTERNS— A CAUSE FOR HOPE

*Meaning making is the activity of composing a sense of the connections among things: a sense of pattern, order, form, and significance. To be human is to seek coherence and correspondence.*[109]

In the early years, one of the things that made this illness worse was that its symptoms moved in and out and around my body seemingly at random, with no discernible rhyme or reason. I could not tie them to anything specific. A plus B did not equal C in this puzzle—a frustrating situation that made me feel as if there was nothing I could do on my own behalf.

Then, in about year two or three of this tangled maze, something changed. It began with something a good friend said to me. After faithfully accompanying me to a number of doctor's appointments and having heard the results of many tests, she said, "Julie, I just don't think you have a disease that will kill you, because if you did, it would have shown up by now. You have had every test in the book, for heaven's sake." Her words rang true. I trusted them. And while the illness still had no name, the realization that it probably would not kill me made it possible to relax a little. When fear had subsided enough, I could settle down to give my attention to listening to this disease, instead of just batting the symptoms away.

## PATTERNS MEAN AGENCY

Lo and behold, one day, out of the fog, barely discernible shapes began to appear, and hope saw a crack in the door. I began to notice that the symptoms were not completely random; they often presented themselves in patterns. Chaos, which had seemed all pervasive, was punctuated with some predictable rhythms. Oh, joy!

I could sweep my floor for about ten minutes before myalgia cropped up in my neck and back, but if I violated that early warning sign and pushed the limit by even a little bit, a migraine roared in, along with searing eye pain and dizziness. At that point, there was no stopping the flood—muscle weakness, fever, chest wall and glandular pain, along with excruciating exhaustion swept in. However, if I lay down immediately, at the first sign of myalgia, the other symptoms could be avoided. In other words, there were layers to this illness; some symptoms were warning signs; others were all-out recrimination.

The ray of hope grew stronger as I began to see that many of these symptoms could be tied directly to overexertion and inadequate sleep. If I so much as walked anywhere that had even the slightest incline to its grade, or got even a half hour too little sleep, my body leapt up in mutiny. If I stayed upright too long, my nervous system would crackle, tingling erupting in my fingers and toes. Vision problems were the scariest symptom of all. But if I lay down regularly and padded even the smallest activity with rest, I could shore up small islands of time without pain.

Here was another discovery, and an odd one at that. It was two to three days after I had exerted more energy than my central nervous system could handle that the shoe would drop, not the same day, or even the following day, as normally happens with physical exertion and overuse of muscles. If, on a Sunday, for example, I tried to vacuum my living room on less than twelve hours of sleep, a few symptoms would rush in immediately, headaches and nausea—challenging enough, to be sure, but a whole battalion of other debilitating symptoms waited for about two days before they roared in. The delayed reaction had an unnerving calm preceding it, like the eerie silence that often precedes a storm, because I knew the quiet was deceiving. I needed to pay absolute attention to the rumble of thunder in the distance. Sure enough, by Tuesday morning I would be vomiting violently, totally flattened. Again. On the hopeful side, if I stuck rigidly to my body's limits, I could bank energy, could store enough up to buy me more maneuverability.

## FRAGILE HOPE

Understanding these patterns, and learning that other people shared them, had a noticeable impact on me. My defenses, constricted by tension, began to ease; it was like finding a handlebar to grip at the deep end of the pool. Bright hope it was not. Even so, a small range of movement opened *within* the illness, offering enough maneuverability to make a difference. This fed hope.

It was oddly reassuring to see that even a searing disease that had burned away the last stalks of my earlier illusions about dependable health had causes and effects to be deciphered. This meant actions had consequences. The right choices led to miniscule periods of steadier health; the wrong choices took it away. All was not chaos!

Still, like tender new shoots, these fragile gifts of health needed the utmost protection; otherwise no sooner had they appeared than they quickly left the scene—again. Like trick birthday candles with little charges in them, just when I thought I had blown hard enough to extinguish the whole lot, the flames would sputter to life again, first on just one candle, but then on another and another, until suddenly the whole cake was aflame, its surface frosted in a layer of wax. All my blowing had been for naught.

## CONFIRMATION: THIS DISEASE HAS A NAME— I AM NOT ALONE (OR CRAZY)

Amid this discouragement something else widened the channel to hope. As I mentioned in chapter 3, I came across a newsletter in which the dozen or more symptoms that I had been experiencing were clustered together under a heading called CFIDS, an acronym encapsulating three sometimes overlapping diseases: chronic fatigue, fibromyalgia, immune dysfunction syndrome. This beast had a name! While its cause(s) is still unknown, and its treatment elusive, what is clear, from both those suffering from it and those in medical research trying to understand it, is that it impacts virtually every system in the body: the central nervous system, musculoskeletal system, digestive system, hormonal system, endocrine system, and more.

I began to discover books on the subject that named *my* experience. There was Kat Duff's *The Alchemy of Illness*, Susan Griffin's *What Her Body Thought*, and a riveting essay in *The New Yorker* by writer Laura Hillenbrand. Susan Griffin gives voice to the all-encompassing breakdown of systems wrought by this illness:

> With [CFIDS] the medical inventory is so long it verges on the comical. The image that comes to mind is of a dilapidated house whose every system fails; the same night that a pipe bursts, the electricity short-circuits, and besides the darkness, there is no way to power a pump—or even, given that telephones require electricity, call for help.[110]

A recent article in the *Los Angeles Times* reports that chronic fatigue syndrome is actually caused by genetic mutations that impair the central nervous system's ability to adapt to increased stress.[111] According to a major new study by the Center for Disease Control and Prevention (CDC):

> Small changes in many of the genes in the brain prevent the nervous system from rebounding from everyday stress and, less frequently, stronger insults, eventually triggering a cascade of responses that leaves the patient severely

debilitated. . . . This is the first credible evidence for a biological basis for the symptoms. . . . People with CFIDS are as impaired as people with muscular sclerosis or AIDS or who are undergoing chemotherapy for cancer.[112]

"A cascade of responses" is right. While naming the illness was hardly equivalent with controlling it, at least it offered clues as to the beast's nature. Knowing even that much increased the possibilities of aiming various remedies at it. Let me claim, once again, the integral relationship between hope and help. Where there's the possibility of help, however remote, there is hope, and without it, hope sags demonstrably. Help and hope are conjoined twins, whose major organs are shared and indivisible.

## A BARGAINER'S HOPE

In the first few years of this illness, my hope was still a bargainer's hope. I tried more or less to cut a deal with the beast. "If I do this, you will do that, right?" I said to him. "If I restrain myself here, you will do likewise, yes?" The beast was still the boss, to be sure, but I was at least in a conversation with my opponent, and this made a huge difference. I needed to feel myself an agent, not a victim.

The poet Jane Kenyon said of the times her manic depression lifted that "it felt like being pardoned for a crime I did not commit."[113] Even when the symptoms let up, I remained on guard, because if I did not do this, I had to learn over and over the hard way that whenever I got to thinking that the interludes of relief would last, the beast dragged me down the hill again, my body in his mouth, puncture marks in my head. So I speak my gratitudes quietly and go about my daily business, paying "him" his due.

Having said all this, it might be hard to believe that, even after years of debilitating symptoms, I tried to discount this illness. Yet it's true. I wanted so badly to relegate the beast to the sidelines and not have to give him the time of day. But it was *the* reality in my life, and my dreams made sure I admitted that. They pushed denial aside and rang the bell of truth—presenting me with exaggerated pictures of how the disease was registered in my psyche and spirit so that I could not miss it.

I dreamt, for example, about a young man named John, whom I had actually met while working in a prison thirty years ago. His future had been totally cut off and carried away by a prison sentence while merely a teenager, not yet twenty. I also dreamt about my aunt Mary, who spent nearly two decades with a most hideous version of Alzheimer's disease, institutionalized because of it. These dreams screamed the truth: despite my attempts to cordon off illness, I felt confined and diminished in a total way.

# 23. HOW HOPE RETURNS

*When despair for the world grows in me*
*And I wake in the night at the least sound*
*In fear of what my life and my children's lives may be,*
*I go and lie down where the wood drake*
*Rests in his beauty on the water and the great heron feeds.*
*I come into the peace of wild things.*[114]

## BEING IN THE NATURAL WORLD

For most of my adult life, I have had the good fortune to have the kind of work that has allowed me to exercise outdoors, at least briefly, in the late afternoon. This is because the courses I teach meet at night, when the midlife students in our program are not working. When I worked in churches, I could justify leaving in the late afternoon because of all the evening meetings. This pattern began when I joined the jogging club as a teenager, logging hundreds of miles along the country roads surrounding my family's home. It continues, today, in the perambulations I make, alone or with a friend, around the city lakes of Minneapolis. Even in Minnesota's dramatic weather, I would far rather be outside than inside if given a choice, even if it's ten below zero in January, or over one hundred degrees in July.

Living in the land of ten thousand lakes (and numerous rivers), we Minnesotans joke that there must be something in the reptilian brain that is renewed in the act of circling a lake, because so many of us do it. We get a lot of problems solved out there. What is it about moving physically outside that has restorative power? I cannot say exactly, but it does.

This rhythm, this small sanctuary in the day when I travel these familiar paths, has been more about restoring the soul than about exercise. It has been a lifeline. I recognize a pattern in what happens interiorly for me when I walk or bike or, in years past, when I was able to run around a lake.

Here is the pattern. When I start out, I am often removed from myself, having spent all my energy ensconced in a task, preparing for class, or hurrying around town on this or that errand. The act of walking engages the body in such a way that the mind is free to pour out its contents. No longer tethered to a project, no longer forced to focus, all these thoughts and feelings come spilling forth like a geyser. All sorts of things swim up to the surface of consciousness and present themselves. I am suddenly face-to-face with sadness, for example, which is something of a surprise. I didn't know I felt sad. Or I bump into anger and wonder, what is *this* about? There are other emotions, too: joy, grief, gratitude, bewilderment, and a whole bevy of thoughts to match. I see how fixated I am on a problem—the cost of removing a tree in my backyard, for example. Or a student's grade. Why did I give her a B+ when I gave this other person an A? Now that I can watch my mind, I am shocked by how busy it is, dashing here and there, rendering judgments, solving problems, reacting as if everything were an emergency. All of this is to say that the first mile or more of walking is, for me, about clearing out.

By about the second mile, when the mind and emotions have gotten enough air time, the natural world can work its wonders. I am, finally, available to them. A space has been hollowed out for receptivity. There is room in me for seeing, hearing, smelling, savoring, appreciating. I notice what I have flown by for days—the canopy of Dutch elms and tall cottonwoods that stand like benevolent sentinels, watching over our neighborhood. The surprise of birdsong in the bracing winter air. The enduring willow trees, hugging the lakeshore's banks with their large, underground roots. All of this shifts things in me. Surrounded by the wide-open prairie sky, my small self is taken up by something larger. In the presence of beauty and its harmonies, the fierce edges of my little ego relax, and I am given back to life as the gift it is. All the energy that has been spent on achieving gives way to beholding. The pushy voice with the whip that says, "Get going, get doing, get reading, writing, cleaning, producing, proving your worth," sits down, tempered. And what happens to the ego in those sixty minutes can take months and years of meditation to achieve. It moves out of the driver's seat and takes its proper place in back.

While walking the lake, I find that things find their proper perspective, and hope has often been reinvigorated. What seemed overwhelming only an hour ago does not seem so now. Things have shaken out. I see more clearly what I can control and what I cannot. I often have a better sense of what I might do in relation to the project or problem or person I am thinking about, and whom I might ask for help. I carry the burden more lightly.

While the lakes and the Midwestern prairies have their own particular beauty, the truth is that the place where my body and soul feel most at home is in the Pacific Northwest. Some of this is about family, of being in the place I grew up, but something else makes for this belonging. It is the land and water. There, in the tides' endless rhythms; there, in the shadow of the Cascade and Olympic Mountains, studded pink in the sunset; there, where two-hundred-foot cedars stand, their long arms draped with leaves and moss like the cassock of a giant monk; there, where harbor seals rise up out of the sea with their large inquiring eyes and prehistoric faces; there, I come home. There, my root system gets regrounded. I respond to the land at every level. There, beauty has a palpable presence that gets all the way into my bones.

The other distinguishing aspect of the landscape in Washington is heights. There are heights—views! I rarely feel like I can get up high enough to look out over the landscape in Minnesota. Our family place sits on a hundred-foot bank overlooking the ocean—a perfect perch from which to gaze out. For me, a different kind of wisdom is available when I have a view. It helps me take the long view of things and to remember that everything, every relationship, every project, every healing process has an arc to it. I am taken up into Something More, a larger rhythm, a larger force field, weaving me in its folds.

In Minnesota the weather is a force to be reckoned with, but around Puget Sound, other things are large—sea, mountains, orcas, eagles. It is also replete with memorable sounds: the loud incoming tide, with its strong attendant current, the wind in the trees, the screeching kingfisher punishing me for entering its territory, the unappealing gawking sound of eagles, the regular slap of a small fishing boat against the water, the wondrous breathing of an orca whale. All of this takes me up. The constricting edges of myself that have been exacerbated by pain and illness finally unfurl.

Once, when I wondered if I might be dying, I spent several weeks lying prone on the sofa of my family's cabin at the water's edge. It was here that I realized it would not be a bad thing at all to dissolve and become one with the eagles, the cedars, and the ocean spray, to become one with what is ageless and eternal, to become one with earth. There, I gazed most evenings at the sunset above Cypress Island. I memorized the contours of that island's topmost ridge. The fir, pine, hemlock, and cedar that make up its outline look like the teeth of a giant's comb. All summer, I gazed and gazed, and it was as if the landscape answered back. I am held up here. Upheld here. I belong here.

When you are sick, you feel on the sidelines, out of the game. You feel like an observer, not a participant. Everything happens around you, but you are separate from it. Pain constricts. It forces you to assume a protective posture and, in so doing, collapses your attention into the confines of your body, or the four walls of your bedroom. This sharpens the boundaries between self and everything else. Even though the healing properties of beauty did not heal me physically, they still worked on me. Being in the presence of beauty reminds you that your pain is not all there is.

# Savoring What's Right with the World

It would be nice if a person could simply go out and automatically find some hope, like you would go off to a bakery to buy a loaf of bread. While hope cannot be plucked directly like that, we can be aware of the patterns in our lives by which hope seems to return, and get ourselves in position to receive it. By this I mean there are habits of heart and mind that nourish hope, habits we can cultivate. One can keep on the lookout for kindness, for example, by staying alert for the gestures of consideration and sympathy between people that restore your faith in our humanity. Conversely, when people's actions and attitudes are disappointing and not a particularly fruitful source of hope, you can turn instead to the beauty and rhythms of the natural world. Regardless of the direction you turn, being alert, open, and attuned to life's wonders opens a channel for hope.

A good friend of mine invites her grandchildren to spend a week every summer with her and her husband at their lake cabin in northern Minnesota. A year or two ago, when her twin granddaughters were about five, one of them had to traipse off to the bathroom in the middle of the night, so Kathy accompanied her. It was a warm, clear, star-studded night, and on their way back to the cabin the child asked her grandmother if she could wish upon a star. "Well, of course," she responded, "what a good idea." The child looked heavenward for a few minutes as they stood there in silence. After a while she came to this conclusion: "Oh, nevamind," she said in the accent of five-year-olds who have trouble pronouncing *r*'s and *l*'s. "It's aweady purfect." Perfect indeed. And a large part of that moment was the child's capacity for wonder.

# Working with the Mind

There are other habits of mind that nourish hope. I am thinking here of the learned skill of remaining faithful to meditation practices that can interrupt punitive thoughts, soften judgmental attitudes, and short-circuit self-critical tapes that play in our heads and poison our outlook. One need not be an addict to know about "stinkin' thinkin'" and the ways our minds can obsess about almost anything, nursing grudges, taking others' inventories, blaming, sulking, justifying one's own behavior, or wallowing in the muck of cynicism.

There are also intentional ways to practice seeing beneath the surface of things to life's underlying goodness. The year I turned fifty I took as my spiritual practice the commitment to take one picture a day for the entire year. I wanted to capture the daily wonders of my "one, wild, and precious life." Whether it was a snapshot of my beloved house over the course of a year's seasons, the neighbor's lilac bush bursting into bloom, the warmth of a friend's face across the table, or my car mechanic, Nick, at Isles Auto (who has reincarnated my old beater car numerous times)—I snapped pictures of the many people who make my world go round. The picture-a-day practice succeeded in helping me cultivate appreciation, admiration, and an awareness of how much quiet goodness graces my days, a healing counterpoint to the horrors chronicled on the news.

In difficult times, hunting for hope requires sheer force of will. Barbara Kingsolver gives voice to this:

> In my own worst seasons I've come back from the colorless world of despair by forcing myself to look hard, for a long time, at a single glorious thing: a flame of red geranium outside my bedroom window. And then another: my daughter in a yellow dress. And another: the perfect outline of a full, dark sphere behind the crescent moon. Until I learned to be in love with my life again. Like a stroke victim retraining new parts of the brain to grasp lost skills, I have taught myself joy, over and over again.[115]

Some of us are fed by particular places or activities that hold the possibility of hope. We make the trek to a favorite spot on the river with our fishing pole, climb a favorite peak, put on our favorite music, or engage the creative process with our paintbrush, pen, or musical instrument. In each case, there is a willingness to patiently reside on the lip of hope—to bid its return, elusive though hope may be, by remaining on the bridge between one's current circumstances and the opening to something larger, hidden in the vicinity.

## HOPE'S BEGINNINGS IN GRIEF, LAMENTATION, AND ANGER

At other times, the path back to hope begins in lamentation or in grief. I distinctly remember something a visiting writer said to a group of students in our Master of Fine Arts program in writing more than a dozen years ago. The author of a mystery and several novels, she had been asked to talk about her own creative process as an artist. Her husband had recently left her, and she was bearing the whole weight of parenting three little boys alone. She told us that on weekday mornings, she would leave her children with their grandparents or a babysitter and will herself to her studio, where she would try to write for a few hours. In order to tap her creativity, buried within all that angst, she had to be present to the emotional truth of things, which was that she was completely devastated, furious about her husband's departure, worried for her children, grief stricken about the breakup of her family, and unsure how it would be possible to move forward. There was no way to leap over all that. So her starting place on most of those mornings when pen touched the page was a torrent of grief. She would complain and cry, rant and rave, wailing, as it were, through writing—page after page soaking up all that heavy emotion like a sponge. What she came to see was that when she gave grief its due, eventually its heft and weight shifted, and a passageway emerged that took her beyond pain to a gentler place. Yet it required considerable work to delve into pain, rather than skirt around it. That itself was a discipline. As the days wore on, however, hope broke out, like rays of sunlight emerging after a downpour.

When I worked in a treatment center for kids with drug and alcohol addiction, I had a front-row seat to the emergence of hope out of anguish. Our teenage clients were divided into three groups: the blue squad was for the aggressive teenagers who had been perpetrators; the green squad was for the wily ones who had gone through treatment more than once and had figured out the system; and the red squad was for those who were generally passive and withdrawn, often the victims of abuse.

One day, a blond-haired young woman in the red squad, who had been sexually abused by every male member of her family (and who until then had hidden in shame behind her hair, face looking down at the floor), rose up out of her humiliation in such a surprising way that it left her counselors, peers, and chaplain speechless. When it was her turn to speak about her progress in the program, she did something uncharacteristic for her. She began, seated among a circle of peers, her voice quivering at first, but gaining strength, and she stood up on her chair. She said she did not deserve the abuse she had been victim to and was not going to spend the rest of her life in its shadow. "I deserved more than this," she proclaimed in a voice rising to a full crescendo. "No one should have to experience what I have! I am a good person! I deserve better! These men in my family are sick. This has been shit! I want my life back, dammit!"

Those of us who were witness to this unexpected flowering of a young person, who was finally able to give voice to her anger and rage, felt tremendous hope for her. If she could allow herself this unrestrained emotion, could see and give voice to her own self-worth—apart from what had happened to her—there was hope—real hope for her recovery from addiction, and hope that her sense of self would begin to blossom. She could articulate the necessity of boundaries in human relationships, and she knew that crossing them was a deep violation.

In truth, the headwaters of her hope had their beginnings much earlier, in the first days and weeks of treatment, long before she was conscious of anything changing, and in ways no outsider could have seen. In the tough emotional work that she had done, together with her peers in their respective groups, were the tributaries from which hope grew. Finally, the shame and rage over being sullied by her abusers forced themselves to the surface and burst through her timidity like molten lava. The unleashing of such great passion about what *should not have been* in her life opened the floodgates for hope to wash in.

## Hope's Surprise Return

Sometimes hope comes back as sheer surprise, and you could not have said exactly how or why it returned. A good night's sleep somehow righted what was off balance. Or someone at work told you a joke that had you chuckling all day, and in the wake of humor's healing a dozen minor difficulties lay down to rest. The Minnesota writer Patricia Hampl gives voice to the surprise of hope's return on a dull winter day in the northland, in a parking ramp, of all places.

> Standing by the parking ramp elevator
> a week ago, sunk, stupid with sadness.
> Black slush puddled on the cement floor,
> the place painted a killer pastel
> as in an asylum.
> A numeral "1," big as a person,
> was stenciled on the cinder block:
> Remember your level.
> The toneless bell sounded.
> Doors opened, nobody inside.
> Then, who knows why, a rod of light
> at the base of my skull flashed
> to every outpost of my far-flung body—
> I've got my life back.
> It was nothing, just the present moment
> occurring for the first time in months.
> My head translated light,
> my eyes spiked tears.
> The awful green walls, I could have stroked them.
> The dirt, the moving cube I stepped into—
> it was all beautiful,
> everything that took me up.[116]

In my own case with illness, from time to time the tiger lets go its choke hold and I sail, blessedly, into a harbor of steadier health. Sometimes for hours, even a whole day, the constant static of symptoms dies down and I am overwhelmed by how spacious life feels. As pain's static ceases, energy runs clear, moving outward, uninterrupted. Hemmed in no longer, my defenses relax. I no longer have to calculate, minute to minute, hour to hour, what is possible or not possible, depending on my pain or energy level. All these years I have had to test the terrain, as blind people maneuver by tap-tap-tapping the area around them with a cane. When I am let loose from such minute measuring, I feel unspeakable relief. It is as if a dirty windshield had been suddenly made clean after years of driving through prolonged and dangerous storms on rutted country roads, with dirt-caked windows, barely able to see, though the windshield wipers work furiously, unable to keep up.

It seems odd to say, but what is most noticeable in health is how quiet my body seems—organs, muscles, nerves, and rivers of blood hum quietly, working happily together in unison, though I know from neurological exams that they are actually quite loud. My own inner motor (what the Chinese call chi) is all revved up and ready to go. Oh, blessed health, invisible jewel in the crown of blessing— you're back!

# 24. SHELTERING HOPE

*Whenever we take it into our heads to express hope in Spanish, we say: abrigamos esperanzas ("we shelter hope").* [117]

When hope is still new and delicate, it may need to be sheltered. Like human babies, who are consummately vulnerable and helpless at birth, so too are the nascent stirrings of hope before they have been tested, or victories before they are consolidated. I have learned this the hard way. Ever eager to share good news with those who inquire about how I'm feeling, when hope has stuttered, then flickered into flame with bursts of steadier health, I have announced it to anyone within shouting distance. Now I know to be more cautious and hold back from proclamations, not because these spurts of health are not worth celebrating, but because they do not yet have deep roots, and they cannot be counted on. If they are pushed too hard, they will fall back. I have been a slow learner in this regard, and it took a number of relapses to understand that my health still needs to be incubated, like a newborn still slightly underweight.

When I think of vulnerable young shoots that require a protective, hovering presence, I think of how my grandmother tended her bulbs. She got them started down in her basement in late winter, long before they were forced to defend themselves from the erratic spring weather. They began stirring to life down there, and had they been exposed too soon, they would surely have shriveled up and died. She waited until the roots had taken hold in their beds of soil and her garden was ready to receive them. Only then were they transplanted.

What is true of flowers and children is also true of projects and dreams: if you yank up the roots to measure how they're doing all the time, you are not doing them any favors. You have to trust the direction of the process, even when the soil is dark and you're blind to what is happening underground. One of hope's adversaries is asking for proof of its vitality all the time, rather than letting it take shape in its own time. "It's always too soon to go home," writes cultural historian Rebecca Solnit. "Most of the great victories continue to unfold, unfinished in the sense that they are not yet fully realized, but also in the sense that they continue to spread influence."[118]

There are countless ways to shelter hope. The parent or teacher who will not give up on a troubled child is doing so. The scientist who persists at his research when the results are only faintly promising is harboring hope. The ill person willing to stay with an experimental medication to give it time and the benefit of doubt is, too. So is the diplomat who will not leave the bargaining table when there's even the thinnest shred of possibility for a deal. Hope sometimes requires this kind of container.

Sheltering hope means cupping in my memory the experiences of being free from pain, even when those stretches are ever so brief. When pain and symptoms come roaring back, I try to hold on to the truth that there really was a span of time when I felt healthy and had more energy, even if it was only a day, or a portion of a day. Surely, I tell myself, if it happened once or twice, it can happen again. One day my body will free itself of illness's grip. I try to stay anchored in this truth, holding on to health's "having-been-ness."

# 25.  STORIES CAN BE MEDICINE

*Stories have to repair the damage that illness has done to the ill person's sense of where she is in life, and where she may be going. Stories are a way of redrawing maps and finding new destinations.*[119]

In the first months and years of being sick, I reached primarily for one kind of medicine—that which could temper pain and help me sleep. This included the heavy-hitting narcotics Vicodin and Percocet (which often did not work), and sleep medications like Trazodone and Amitriptyline. As the years wore on, I began to seek another kind of medicine, that which could help me bear the illness spiritually and emotionally.

We human beings cannot stand chaos for long. It makes us crazy. Physically, chaos was wreaking havoc in my body. I was the unwitting host to a raft of indiscriminate symptoms that flashed here, now there, like random strikes of lightning. I needed a way to "hold" what was happening to me, needed a way to frame the experience in a larger context. This may sound like an intellectual exercise. It is not. It is an emotional and spiritual need, every bit as essential as the need for pain relief. Why? Because, in the absence of meaning, hope is lost.

Whatever our circumstances, if we feel that our lives are "hung, like a picture, within a larger frame,"[120] and that we are more than a separate self dangling in midair, it can make the intolerable slightly more tolerable. The "great stories" create just such a frame. I am not talking here about just any story, but about the religious and mythic stories that have served as maps of the human experience for centuries. Think the people of Israel stuck in the wilderness of exile. Think Jesus' death and resurrection. Think Gautama Buddha waking up to the unacceptable poverty around him. Consider the Odysseus and Penelope story of Greek legend.

Grand stories such as these do more than give shape to our experience. They "are the self's medium of being."[121] They say: people have been this way before, and they have left field notes about how to negotiate the territory. Stories offer reference points, glimpses of the patterns we can expect, and clarity about what is required of us on a soul level. Like force fields, they draw the broad array of life experience into them, giving order to disorder and holding our fears. By encircling our hardships, they put boundaries around them, serving as a vessel in which to contain them.

As to where stories begin, that is a good question. Writer Susan Griffin suggests that "in a sense, the drama of the body provides the model for all narrative. As far as I can surmise, the mysterious need for narration is seated in the body. What else is a cry of pain or pleasure but a small story?"[122]

One of the realizations that dawned on me fairly early in my illness was that sincere as people were in their questions about how I was feeling, the illness story throws a wrench into most people's expectations. We as a culture are reluctant to admit that our lives have gone badly in some significant way. Consequently, chaos stories do not feel very good. People are not sure what to say when I can't offer them a version of the conventional format: "Yes, I have been really sick, but thankfully things are getting better, and surely my future will be bright." So they are left with a gaping hole in the narrative that feels uncomfortable, and it's a hole I cannot fix.

In my quest for meaning and hope despite my illness, something else began to bother me, though I could not name it for a while. It simmered as a general annoyance for some time before its cause finally crystallized. This is what angered me: though Western medicine had no answers for me, did not even diagnose my illness let alone offer remedies for it, the medical narrative had the power to trump all other stories. Yet I knew that more was involved than the medical story could tell. I needed a way to see both the facts of my medical situation and the larger soul situation. And mythic stories do this. They insert themselves into the narrative wreckage caused by a crisis. They stand up to traditional Western medicine and say: "Wait just a minute here; there is something else going on!" That is why a story can be medicine.

## INANNA

The story most helpful to me in illness was that of Inanna, the Babylonian queen and perhaps the world's first goddess of recorded history. It was her descent to the underworld that captured my imagination.[123]

I vaguely remembered that Inanna had to pass through a number of gates in her journey through the underworld, and at each successive gate she was forced to surrender something. There are varied interpretations of these losses. The first item to go in this stripping process was her crown, symbolic of her nobility and majestic stature. Then followed her royal robes, representing her personality and public identity. After that she was required to sacrifice her necklace, representing a bond between Inanna and the gift giver, perhaps an erotic bond at that. Then her breastplate was handed over, robbing her of her defenses and the masculine attributes in herself. Letting go of her lapis measuring rod left her without a way to find her bearings. The release of her jewelry, that is, her material riches, was followed by the double strand of beads over her heart, which represented her wisdom and compassion. Then, having been stripped completely, she had nothing, and was nothing but the desire to begin again. (Talk about being completely reduced and sundered! Isn't this what life can do?) But even that is not the end of it for Inanna. As a further, hellish denouement, she was hung up on a meat hook like a piece of flesh!

Not to be overly dramatic here, but that's about how I felt, lying prone on the sofa on a beautiful summer day for the fifth or sixth year in a row, in the midst of another debilitating relapse. My head and eyes hurt from sharp, throbbing pain. Waves of dizziness and fever rolled through me day and night. My muscles were weak and shaky. My chest wall hurt, and my jaw hurt. I felt excruciating exhaustion, which sleep did not alleviate. At one point I vomited so violently the whites of my eyes were completely red.

With Inanna's story working in me in this grim state, I asked my artistic father to draw a series of gates on wide sheets of sketch pad paper. Under each gate I named a sacrifice demanded by my illness: trust in the dependability and strength of my body, which until then had been a remarkably resilient and faithful vessel; the ability to plan, not knowing whether the tortuous fatigue and other pain would allow me to get out of bed or not; a shift in personality and outlook from an energetic and optimistic person to a cautious and dour one hovering, protectively, over a depleted body. Any and all exercise was out of the question, a bitter pill for an athletic person with such love of moving. On every count I felt diminished. Hope had to backpedal and wait in the wings while renunciation took hold. It was the requirement that filled the whole canvas, and there was no seeing beyond it. However, even though hope was fragile and in retreat, it was alive, awaiting possibilities that had not yet been revealed.

As for the contours of my own underworld, it was a labyrinthine path that wound through the offices of dozens of specialists—infectious disease specialists, neurologists, specialists in lung conditions and pain, chiropractors, naturopaths, endocrinologists, eye specialists, herbologists, homeopaths, energy healers, acupuncturists, an ob-gyn physician well schooled in hormonal imbalances, and so on. This path included endless examinations, batteries of tests, and experiments that led to dead ends. I kept bumping into walls. Help and health were hidden at the end of some long, elusive corridor whose entrance I could not find. I began to lose confidence that I would ever find help, and without it there was precious little hope.

At the time I could not have said exactly how or why, but drawing parallels with Inanna's story was strangely strengthening. While it changed nothing physically about my situation, her story spelled out what my body and soul were experiencing. It embedded my own chaos story in a universal narrative, which made the experience something I could bear. Rather than discount the hellish dimensions of my own illness, which would serve only to distance me from my body's truth, it gave me permission to say how bad things really were. Yes: it had been *that* dramatic. Yes: it had been *that* costly. Just as Inanna's descent to the underworld had demanded everything of her, this illness has demanded everything of me. While I cannot explain just how this works, I do know that this story allowed me to experience the truth of my situation more fully than I could have without it.

This ancient tale makes the experience of plummeting against one's will into a deep void come alive. It says: this is how descent can feel. It says: maybe, just maybe, you will emerge back into the light of day. This is no small gift when your own defining story seems to have collapsed around you. It is as if there is no relationship between you and the Author of life, a conclusion that for me would have been too much to bear. This is where depression and resignation can begin, or, in my case, a furious impatience.

Rather than discounting the hellish dimensions of my own illness, which would serve only to distance me from my true self and my body's truth in the process, it gave me permission to say how bad things really were and to name each and every significant loss. Ironically, taking my predicament this seriously strengthened hope because it honored the truth of my experience.

# 26.  IN PRAISE OF COPING

*Coping is quiet. There is no fanfare, no parades. Just a quiet task aimed at emotional well-being, if not survival, pursued in subdued and sober tones and spoken in whispers, not in shouts. The formula for successful coping rests in the eye of the beholder. There is no magic. We simply know it when we live it.*[124]

oping is not only the province of the sick. It is the plain but necessary staying power to stay in life and go forward. This capacity to contend with a tough situation, to struggle vigorously with an adversary, whatever or whoever that might be, is the only way hope can remain alive. It is ordinary, essential, and some days, miraculous.

At times, life is an endurance contest. I saw this truth up close when I worked as a chaplain in a prison in northeast Philadelphia. After introducing myself to an inmate, I would invariably ask him how he was doing. A frequent response would be, "I'm dealin'," which meant: "I am getting by, but just barely." While coping may be worlds away from thriving, finding the strength to endure can require all you've got. We reach to find the strength we need to meet each day, whatever life delivers.

## CERTAIN THINGS CAME NATURALLY

In my longest days with chronic illness, I needed every coping skill I could muster. By this I mean the emotional and mental resources needed to bear the burden of my body's dire condition. It helped that I already had a well-developed sense of determination and persistence, which I credit in part to being an athlete. As mentioned before, I was a competitive tennis player, the number one player on my high school and college teams. During the summers in my seminary years, I, along with my eight able assistants, taught nearly eleven hundred people to play tennis on the park and high school courts of Spokane. I also loved to run, ski, swim, and bike. Competing and winning were not the point for me; it was the moving itself that made me feel fully alive. Running in the late afternoons down along the Spokane River connected me to myself. It brought me close to my own voice, to what *I* thought, what *I* felt, what *I* loved. I "wrote" some of my best papers between my dorm room and the river.

I also come from people who value hard work. This enabled me to hang in there and not give up on the possibility of healing when it did not come right away. Since I am a single breadwinner, I needed to draw on these attributes of necessity, to work in spite of pain. In that regard, here is what coping "looked like" in my daily life. Instead of canceling a class, I would lie down on the floor of my office beforehand, dim the lights to near darkness, and concentrate on breathing, in an effort to conserve every ounce of energy I could and make it through the evening. I canceled many work trips, but when I did have to travel on planes, I would take my migraine medicine, prop my head against the window with a pillow, shut my eyes, and hunker down in silence, all systems marshaled to bear pain.

Working with severe limits forced me into an ongoing dialogue with my body, another coping strategy. I would by turns question her, plead with her, and berate her. "Do you think we can go to work today? Or would this be too much?" "Oh, please, don't be dizzy now; wait until I am finished with this presentation." "Give me a break, will you! I got twelve hours of sleep and you are still racked with headaches? What do I have to do to calm you down?"

In crisis, some aspect of our personality that has resided, until then, in the background may come to the fore. Friends and colleagues say there is a fighter spirit in me that illness has flushed out. They say I am fierce about not letting illness claim me entirely. I have been surprised at these responses myself.

While my own tendencies as a driver, striver, "type A" achiever have their drawbacks, I dare say there is also much to commend in them. For one thing, they are reliable. I move quickly into leadership mode in a crisis. I hunt around for new possibilities, circle back around the remedies already tried while casting about for new ones. I am your original "try harder" personality. That is partly what landed me here, in chronic fatigue syndrome's territory, in the first place. There are benefits to this way of being, however. So when I came across this accolade for achievement-oriented types, I cheered:

> Patients with high levels of motivation and goal-seeking behavior process their expectation of benefit as a form of reward. The reward circuits found in the frontal lobes of the brain are rich in dopamine.[125]

# OTHER SKILLS MAY NEED TO BE LEARNED

One of the coping skills I had to develop was the willingness to throw politeness to the wind and have the guts to press medical experts beyond their polite summations and generalizations that gave me nothing to go on, nothing to do on my own behalf. I sat in the office of an infectious disease specialist one dark winter day, flattened by sadness and fatigue. Shooting eye pain pummeled me relentlessly. I had met with this man every few months for more than a year, and while kind, he was perplexed about my condition—the eye pain in particular—and said he knew of no way to help me. Something in me rose up in mutiny there. This was not an adequate answer! Did he not know any eye specialist I might contact? What would he do if he were experiencing this level of pain? What if I was his wife? His daughter? What would he recommend then? As it happened, he did know an eye specialist at the University of Minnesota, a man of some renown, which made it nearly impossible to get an appointment with him. The doctor had his nurse call that office, and ten minutes later I had an appointment scheduled.

Sometimes coping was synonymous with patience and surrender. I would cancel meetings, ask someone to officiate a wedding for me, or teach my class and then lie down in the dark. Or I would prop my head up and will myself to read student papers, resting after each one. At other times the only thing to do was to lie flat and rest.

## ANGER

I have found it vital to claim and express my feelings—to lament and complain, let loose with anger, grief, and disappointment, lest stuffed feelings become a swelling tide of sullen indignation with nowhere to go. As Susan Griffin notes, if these feelings are discounted, the consequence of pretending everything is all right "is an even more subtle inner abandonment," because "the soul is bound up with honesty in some way that cannot, except at great cost, be violated."[126] It's frustrating, confounding, infuriating when little episodes of health flow in, only to be carried quickly out to sea again. When this happens, it is as if a crucial element of my original being, or a fragment of blessing that I so dearly want, is caught in the undertow, pulled just out of reach. Health, a wild and distant thing, refuses to stay.

If a person has a friend or family member who is willing to be alongside him or her in this "place," without being frightened by anger, it's an invaluable gift that strengthens both one's ability to cope and one's hope, because with anything chronic you feel like a burden to others. There is another reason a person's patient presence is so healing: the tedious details of illness can seem boring and stupefying—even to one's self. When you feel free to talk about them, without abbreviating or tempering your comments for fear of weighing the other person down, you "pull a thread through a narrow opening flanked on one side by shame, and on the other by trivia."[127] If no one is available or willing to hear you, you have to let it out alone. Jean Dominique-Bauby says of his own useful anger in the midst of his hellish, locked-in syndrome, "To keep my mind sharp, to avoid descending into resigned indifference, I maintain a level of resentment and anger, neither too much nor too little, just as a pressure-cooker has a safety valve to keep it from exploding."[128]

More often than not, as I register my rage at all of this—and letting fly a stream of expletives is not something I contemplate—it just shoots out of me, gushing like a geyser, exposing hot, bubbling anguish. I find myself in a screaming spasm at a small frustration when I know it's the illness that's the true source of my fury—anguish about the too-muchness and too-longness of this stupid illness, which is never over. Anguish represents spiritual loss. It announces violation. Something one holds dear has been negated, and it must be named. Pi, the protagonist in Yann Martel's novel, has it right when he says:

> When your animal has trespassed upon your territory, be unflagging in your outrage. Whether you have fled to your safe haven off the lifeboat or retreated to the back of your territory on the lifeboat, START BLOWING YOUR WHISTLE AT FULL BLAST AND IMMEDIATELY TRIP THE SEA ANCHOR.[129]

Sometimes I tap into this stream of frustration best while moving. There is something about the physical momentum of walking, biking, or even raking the lawn that accesses powerful emotions, stirring up the juices. While it may be cathartic, even strengthening, to express anger, it has little impact on the illness itself, since disease does not understand spite. Flailing away at it is about like telling a hurricane to "get the hell out of here!" Even so, expressing it is a form of truth-telling that seems essential.

## HOPE DOES NOT ALWAYS LOOK BUOYANT

What these ruminations on coping reveal is that sometimes hope does not look or feel buoyant. Sometimes it may not even seem like hope, but it is—this capacity to hold on for dear life in the nitty-gritty details of making it through an hour, a day, a month, a season, with some sense, however dim, of a way forward. It is clutching, gripping, white-knuckling it, not soaring.

That's what hope is, no shining thing but a kind of sustenance, plain as bread, the ordinary thing that feeds us. . . . Hope has to do with continuing, that's all: thin stuff . . . which—looked at in this light—seems really neither thin nor plain, but miraculous. What keeps us going? Some native will to live, as much as the stuff out of which we're made as blood or bone.[130]

Hope comes in many brands, and coping encompasses any and all of the strategies one can muster to remain in hope's vicinity.

People in AA talk about taking things day by day. In illness, a day can seem like a lifetime. I found it more helpful to think in terms of making it from hour to hour, or even minute to minute. As the prison inmates taught me, you "deal" with trouble any way you can. If your wings are injured, you may have to run. If you can't run, you have to walk. And if you can't walk, you crawl. If crawling is not possible, then you reach out from within, even if the reaching is no louder than a whimper. Here's the truth of it: sometimes it is not possible to fling yourself out of a ravine. You need something or someone external to lift you. Which brings us, once again, to help, hope's closest ally.

## TAPPING NATURAL TENDENCIES

In truth, I do have hope that help will be forthcoming for those suffering from this condition—in the long run. Why? Because so many people have it (or variations of it), and many in medical research are working on the problem. Surely someone will crack the code sooner or later. In the short term, however, a more cautious and realistic hope is needed. It seems the better side of wisdom to acknowledge that a lasting truce with a wild animal may not be possible. When I forget this, ever so briefly, the beast sends up a roar from the other room, an indication that if I do not factor in his existence, he will come stalking me, exacting stiff penalties for any hint of denial. I know our government says it does not negotiate with terrorists who have kidnapped its own citizens. My own foreign policy is more amenable to deal-making, because the foreigner has taken up residence in me.

It has also helped immeasurably that I have been part of a large circle of love, care, and prayer. I have no doubt that these resources have undergirded me in more ways than I will ever know. In the best of moments, the fruit of this encircling has been an innate trust that heaven knows about this. In other words, though healing may be elusive, I am not dangling loosely in outer space beyond the reach of God. I do not have to shout.

## Being Accompanied

When plateaus of steadiness are reached for days, even weeks at a time, hope soars, and I see how quickly I can forgive this beast. "*Tusand takk*," said my Norwegian grandfather after receiving a gift, "a thousand thanks." "Thanks a million," I say to God, and the whole big sky. "*Thank you* for whatever it was that released me." Like a battered wife who wants mostly for the animal to just leave her house, I have no need to hold grudges or report the abuse to the authorities. They already know about it. Let's just be done with this; get him to leave my premises for good and I will be one happy woman.

## Thought Patterns Matter

Attentiveness to one's thoughts is particularly important in coping with chronic conditions, for when our bodies are unhappy, our minds can be unhappy, too. When my chiropractor, who has reliable intuitive wisdom, suggests that my thinking may be getting in the way of healing, I balk, defensive at first. Yet I know underneath it all that he is right. My mind goes round and round repeating the number of years I've been dragging this ball and chain behind me, "six, seven, getting on toward eight," I repeat, "six, seven, getting on toward eight." My mind is caught in fury. It circles around several thoughts like a dog wound up in its chain. "Will I ever get better? It's been too long now. Will I ever get better? It has been too long now." I wish I could send my mind to detox.

At other times, the problem is just the reverse. When I've been wrung out by pain and fatigue, I frankly don't have the energy to focus, let alone correct my thinking. It's fuzzy and sluggish, like an elderly uncle, barely shuffling forward, his synapses misfiring and groaning as they struggle to get out of neutral. In such times all I can do is to try to be where my body is, and not harangue about it.

My chiropractor does not suggest that I leap into false cheer, but that I loosen my grip on the longevity theme, because

> hopelessness is rooted in structures of thought, feeling, and action that are rigid and inflexible. They are absolutized and repetitive structures that have become so many traps. . . . These absolute structures lead to a sense of endlessness. In short, the way the body talks to the brain powerfully shapes our sense of hope or despair.[131]

Sometimes the best thing to do is to surrender the day and go to bed, hoping that something will shift in my mind during sleep. At other times the simplest of things can bolster hope and thinking along with it: a whole day without head pain, the energy to have someone over for dinner, more buoyancy in my body. In this way, hope unleashes "a domino effect, a chain reaction, each increment making the next increase more feasible. The familiar poetic phrase 'hope flowers' captures this catalytic process."[132] Good sleep impacts the body, which impacts hope, which impacts thought. I worship sleep.

My experience is that it's not enough to try to rationalize one's way to hope; it comes, most often, "as an amalgam of thought and feeling, the feelings created in part by neural input from the organs and tissues."[133] When you feel better, physically, the mind shifts into a different pattern, too.

To put the final point on this theme, how I think of my body matters. Whether I perceive myself to be contending with my body or contending with an illness, whether I see myself surrendering to my body or working to accommodate it or fighting it makes an enormous difference in my ability to cope.

But what's frankly confusing, and aggravating, is trying to discern whether this illness is part of my soul's business, or whether it's getting in the way of my soul's business. Probably both. Why does it matter? Because if I berate my body, which is not itself the problem, I may constrict the flow of healing. My body is trying her level best to right herself. She is my soul's garment in this life, and I need to be her advocate, not her judge. I must partner with her to help free the alien force that has taken up residence in her. Dispatching enmity only adds insult to injury. Ironically, the times I needed the most chutzpah were the times I had the least energy to access it. The times I most needed compassion toward my body, my mind lit out in anger at it, causing a distancing that did not help or heal.

Here is one of life's most poignant paradoxes: our bodies carry our spirit; they are the vehicle through which our souls are grounded in this life. Despite this high calling, however, they are terribly frail. Like a personable old house with an abundance of doors and windows, each human body is porous and permeable, susceptible to terrible storms that blow in and out. While we can do our part to shutter doors and windows against them, none of these gestures is weatherproof. This is why we need to cultivate the voice of wisdom.

## WISDOM'S VOICE

One of the reasons discouragement has not had the final word for me is that a voice of a different quality has visited me from time to time. Just what to call it I do not know. My soul? God's voice? While not easy to describe, I can say that it seemed to come both from within me and from without. Something about its resonance made it trustworthy; it seemed more real than anything else in the material world. When this voice has come through to me, there has been an evenness about it that keeps another line of thinking going on beneath despair.

One summer, when I was sunk again in a relapse, at the time of year when I usually fared much better, this voice said: "You are right, this is awful, but be glad you are on vacation and have time and space to work with it. If it were the first week of school, this would be even harder." You can hear her equanimity. Her levelheadedness. She is pragmatic as an Iowa farm woman, not given to drama. As she calmly reaches for the sandbags, her reasoning goes something like this: "Remember, you have gotten through stretches like this before. Try paying attention to what *you do have*, instead of focusing on the losses. Keep the big picture in mind. You are better than you have been at your worst. This is not a death sentence, though I know how deeply disappointed you are."

What has kept me going? That same drive to live. Stick-to-itiveness. A stubbornness that I cannot completely account for, and a disposition that insists on hope.

## 27. SURPRISING SOURCES OF HOPE

*For the needy shall not always be forgotten,*
*nor the hope of the poor perish forever.*
—Psalm 9:18

Sometimes the source of hope is surprising; it comes from somewhere you would never have thought to look. Here is a story about an unexpected source of hope. Dennis Kucinich, the Democratic representative from Ohio, was the eldest of seven children in a poor family that suffered numerous illnesses and had to move frequently when their father's work changed and as the family grew larger. At one point they lived in their car. Kucinich says of that time:

> It was a Packard. We used to park the car on the edge of the steel mills. We'd use the bathrooms of the taverns in the neighborhood. We'd go and buy bologna sandwiches and white bread and some mustard. . . . In the evenings, I'd look out the window at this big sleeve of flame that was reaching toward the skies, coming out of the . . . oxygen furnace of the steel mill. That pillar of flame gave me a sense of security and hope. It lit the night and it lit the darkness, and this child, with his nose pressed against the window of this car, was just agog at this incredible vision of light just brightening the night. I had a sense that everything was ok.[134]

You just never know where hope may flower. Kucinich's story reminds us once again not to think of hope—or its sources—in rarified ways. It can be carried in simply by the tide of daily routine; as you swept your kitchen floor, sunlight streamed through the windows, and this was enough to lift your spirits. Or preparing a meal and sharing it with a loved one across the dinner table brought hope back.

Etty Hillesum, a young Dutch Jew, recorded in a journal the ways she tried to fortify her soul during the terrifying days that took her and her family to

Auschwitz and to death in November 1943. What kept her spirit alive was something breathtakingly simple— jasmine and the little piece of sky that showed through her prison window.[135]

While we cannot base our primary sources of hope on a diet of surprises, occasionally hope does surprise. It leaks through the cracks of some circumstance that otherwise seemed hopeless. A survivor is found amid the rubble of an earthquake, days after the event. Or events unfold that could not have been predicted by the past; in fact, they represent a sharp break from the past. The Berlin Wall crumbles, for instance. Boris Yeltsin stands atop an armored tank in the center of Moscow, and the top-heavy bulwark of communism collapses like a gigantic supernova. Menachem Begin and Yasir Arafat shake hands on the White House lawn. A bloodless "velvet revolution" brings down communism in the former Czechoslovakia. Thirty million people around the world march in protest of America's invasion of Iraq in March 2003—which, unfortunately, did not stop our president and Congress from declaring war.

# 28. HUMANISTIC HOPE

*What a piece of work is a man! How noble in reason, how infinite in faculty, in form and moving how express and admirable, in action how like an angel, in apprehension how like a god—the beauty of the world, the paragon of animals! And yet to me what is this quintessence of dust?*

—William Shakespeare, *Hamlet*

*When I look at your heavens, the work of your fingers, the moon and the stars that you have established; what are human beings that you are mindful of them, mortals that you care for them? Yet you have made them a little lower than God, and crowned them with glory and honor.*

—Psalm 8:3-5

While we might find it odd to compare ourselves with the angels, if truth be told, most of us would probably prefer to rely on our own human resources to get through life than to ask for help from others or a power beyond ourselves. It is true that we are an amazing species, endowed with many talents and abilities, all of which are laudable: our ingenuity and resourcefulness, our resilience, and our capacity for good. Consider those who donate their organs to other persons they do not even know. Or people who exhibit kindness when their life circumstances should have stripped them of this capacity altogether. At our best we have an extraordinary capacity for generosity and nobility of character. Look what human hands and hearts have wrought, says humanistic hope. Look to the radiance of those exquisite souls who brought to life such stunning attributes as courage and self-sacrifice, wisdom and vision, that they literally take our breath away: Gautama Buddha, Sojourner Truth, Chief Seattle, Fannie Lou Hamer, Anne Frank, Mohandas Gandhi, Eleanor Roosevelt, Nelson Mandela, Aung San Suu Kyi, Etty Hillesum, Rosa Parks, Martin Luther King Jr. Look to geniuses like Albert Einstein and Stephen Hawking. Or to people unknown to the larger world, yet who stand high in your own pantheon of fine souls, who make you proud to be a human being.

Some remember back to that bright day in 1994 when Nelson Mandela emerged from twenty-seven miserable years in prison, in his native South Africa, smiling radiantly, without resentment, but with a magnificence and grandeur that took our breath away and moved a whole world. His dignified demeanor and lack of bitterness were captivating. They served to reinforce his authority as a leader and led to renewed hope about the dismantling of apartheid in South Africa. While that hope is still in the process of being realized, and the vestiges of apartheid linger, Mandela is a tribute to the potential in the human race. He did humanity proud. Here is a man who had every reason to be angry. He was not. Here was a person who could well have held grudges and sought revenge. He did not. His generous and commanding spirit was a central cornerstone in the rebuilding of a new South Africa.

At the root of Mandela's legacy is an essential source of hope, the human capacity for forgiveness. St. Augustine refers to human capacities when he says that hope has two children. The first is anger at the way things are. The second is courage that propels a person to make sure things do not stay as they are. To embrace both is no small feat, for sometimes anger can be so potent that it paralyzes, robbing us of the courage to do anything about the source of anger. We must be angry and impatient about racism, about poverty, about hunger, about homelessness, about homophobia, and about other "isms" that poison us. There is no excuse for them. And yet, anger has its limits. Without the capacity to forgive, the cycle of vengeance always has fuel enough to justify more violence. No human relationship would survive without forgiveness. In its absence we would be drowning in blood.

## THE POWER AND NECESSITY OF FORGIVENESS

The Truth and Reconciliation Commission's process in South Africa, which has become a living example of the possibility of forgiveness and reconciliation that other countries have tried to emulate, was foremost about truth. Its primary focus was on uncovering the atrocities committed there. In the years it took to shape and administer the TRC, its custodians deemed it essential, if healing was to happen, that these truths be publicly named—a reminder that truth and hope must sit side by side. The TRC was not meant as a quick and facile way to expedite "moving on." It was rather a painstaking process of giving voice to victims and their families, of telling and hearing wrenching stories that exposed the perpetrators of evil and revealed how profoundly destructive racism can be.

The Commission agreed to requests for amnesty only when the person making the request admitted wrongdoing. This was a way to make plain the fact that evil is never without an author. While it often grows out of unhealthy systems, human beings are at the center of those systems. Real people make decisions that unleash evil. It is costly to victim and perpetrator alike. Yet in the long run, the reconstruction of society depends upon it. In fact, Archbishop Desmond Tutu notes that "to forgive is indeed the best form of self-interest since anger, resentment and revenge are corrosive."[136] He writes:

> If perpetrators were to be despaired of as monsters and demons, then we were thereby letting accountability go out the window because we were then declaring that they were not moral agents to be held responsible for the deeds they had committed. Much more importantly, it meant that we abandoned all hope of their being able to change for the better. Theology said they still, despite the awfulness of their deeds, remained children of God, with the capacity to repent, to be able to change. As I listened . . . to the stories of perpetrators . . . I realized how each of us has the capacity for the most awful evil—every one of us.[137]

To forgive another person is to let her or him off the hook of your judgment, freeing the other while simultaneously freeing yourself. Forgiveness allows a person to move into the future rather than remain chained to the past. This decision, this interior action, this difficult process, springs hope loose. It reminds us that, while we cannot control other people or their actions, nor can we control much of what happens to us, we can choose how we respond. And when we experience ourselves as a creative force in our own and others' lives, we realize just how potent choices and actions can be.

## Hope Springs from Action

Put another way, hope is not passive. It is a way of moving into the future. In *Life of Pi*, Yann Martel's protagonist, Pi, who is adrift on the sea after a shipwreck, struggles to find the balance between a wistful hope of rescue from some force outside himself, and self-reliance. He says:

> I had to stop hoping so much that a ship would rescue me. . . . Survival had to start with me. . . . A castaway's worst mistake is to hope too much and do too little. To look out with idle hope is tantamount to dreaming one's life away.[138]

After interviewing dozens of people for his reflections on hope, Studs Turkel saw a pattern in them. In story after story about those who came through difficult times, hope rarely trickled down from on high. It usually sprang up with "pressure from below." This is not to say that many did not look to God for their hope. They did. Yet there was an essential human element involved as well. Hope was associated with action, with pressure put upon governments and institutions by trade unions, human rights organizations, religious communities, civil rights activists, and courageous individuals.

It is safe to say that in every era human action has mediated grace. Someone has been willing to stand up for justice. Someone has gone against the grain, risked speaking truth to power, rejected the status quo, slid down a rat hole to join a person suffering there. Some have even been willing to lay down their lives for the sake of others.

One of my graduate students works to involve undergraduates in social justice programs. She sees activism as the best way for people to use their privilege to pass along the message of hope. Activism itself can generate hope because, at its core, it is proposing an alternative. Hope blossoms when people rally around the conviction that things can change and that even a few can make a difference for many. There is a billboard on the freeway connecting Minneapolis and St. Paul. On it are the smiling faces of young children. Above the picture is a fact: there are three thousand homeless children in our state on any given night. Beneath it is a call to action: "We can do better, Minnesota. We must do better." This picture of how things are, distinct from how things ought to be, has galvanized many in our community to work for the end of homelessness here.

When I despair over the unseemly side of human beings, I try to remind myself of an assumption in Buddhist teachings: there are enlightened people (called bodhisattvas) who live among us, here and now, in *this* world. They are filled with love and determination and their consciousness waters the seeds of understanding and compassion in others.

## THE HUMAN CAPACITY TO CHANGE

Hope rests, in part, on our ability as human beings to learn, grow, and change. We can come to question our assumptions. We can come to see things in a different way, thanks to our creative minds and imaginations. We can awaken more fully and be transformed fundamentally. This is a subject so large it dwarfs any description of it. On an individual level, a person's entire way of experiencing life, of thinking, seeing, deciding, believing, and relating, can be altered completely. A longtime alcoholic finds recovery and stays sober, for example. Or a self-centered person discovers her generosity. A lonely person with few interpersonal skills comes alive in a marriage or partnership in an utterly surprising and seemingly miraculous way.

On a societal level, this country came to see racism as unacceptable, and we passed, though not easily, the Civil Rights Bill. Our view of women's roles in the home and workplace have changed dramatically in fifty years. So have our views about mental illness and addiction.

We know that large-scale transformation must happen if we are to have a future as a species. Where are we to start? With a perception that lies at the heart of many daunting challenges of our time. It is the perception that we are solitary entities separate from another and from the earth, our home. This dangerous misperception leads to our need to dominate and control, if not to do battle with or try to eliminate those who are different from us. The primary struggle underlying all our other struggles is "the life-and-death battle between the self and the 'Other.'" And if we could name the most enduring source of hope, it could be "the capacity of some people for genuine self-transcendence, for selfless preference of the Other, sometimes at the cost of life itself."[139]

One of the abiding truths captured across cultures in their myths, tales, and teaching stories is that the person you meet at the beginning of the story is not the same person who returns. Not by a long shot. In the process of failing, suffering, surrendering, and being strengthened, the small self is no longer as self-referential as it used to be. He or she is wiser, kinder, and more awake than before when the story began. In the Greek myths, this is largely because the hero has been tutored by the ancestors and the gods. In the biblical narratives of Judaism and Christianity, it is the action of God in the human soul that brings about transformation. By whatever name we call this fundamental change, the barriers of the little self are breached in the process, and the person experiences connection with her ultimate Source. She or he has embraced a richer, wider perspective on the world and is now more resonant with what Buddhism calls "all sentient beings" and Native Americans call "all our relations."

This process of maturation/transformation can happen for entire communities or countries, not just for individuals. Think of the tree planting in deforested regions of Africa and Haiti. The difficult integration of East and West Germany. The aftermath of war in the Baltic States. Hopefully we in America, who consume a disproportionate amount of the worlds natural resources, can become better relatives to earth's other inhabitants.

One of our country's most prophetic and courageous voices, poet Adrienne Rich, captured the crying need for a breaking open of our nation's self-centeredness in her poem "In Those Years." Though it was written ten years prior to the events of September 11, 2001, it is difficult to read without thinking of the planes that flew into the World Trade Center towers on that day.

## In Those Years

In those years, people will say, we lost track
of the meaning of we, of you
we found ourselves
reduced to I
and the whole thing became
silly, ironic, terrible:
we were trying to live a personal life
and, yes, that was the only life
we could bear witness to

But the great dark birds of history screamed and plunged
into our personal weather
They were headed somewhere else but their beaks and pinions drove
along the shore, through the rags of fog
where we stood, saying I.[140]

If there is any hint of good news in this poem, it is in the possibility that "those years" will be only a chapter of our country's life, and not the whole book. Belonging to an increasingly interconnected world, with its many diversities, requires that we grow beyond narrow allegiance to just our own family, our own tribe, our own nation, and come to a broader sense of family. Our hope as a species lies in this capacity to embrace new forms of patriotism.

I want to draw, again, on the wisdom of a poet, whose poem/elegy gives expression to this. In this poem/elegy, William Stafford addresses the leader of the Oglala Sioux (1849–1877), who was defeated by General George Custer at the Battle of Little Bighorn. Crazy Horse's people were not considered relatives by white people, though they had made this land home long before white people arrived. They were considered enemies to be conquered.

## Report to Crazy Horse

In your life you saw many strange things,
and I will tell you another: now I salute
the white man's flag. But when I salute
I hold my hand alertly on the heartbeat
and remember all of us and how we depend
on a steady pulse together. There are those
who salute because they fear other flags

or mean to use ours to chase them:
I must not allow my part of saluting
to mean this. All of our promises,
our generous sayings to each other, our
honorable intentions—those I affirm
when I salute. At these times it is like
shutting my eyes and joining a religious
colony at prayer in the gray dawn
in the deep aisles of a church.[141]

There are many examples of organizations whose allegiance is to humanity as a whole. I think of Doctors Without Borders—*Médecins Sans Frontiéres*, their French name. Members of this group bring humanitarian medical relief around the world. Many patients tell these doctors that they have never seen a qualified doctor or received treatment before. We could call out together other organizations that share this stance: Amnesty International, Habitat for Humanity, the Nonviolent Peace Force, Care International, the Red Cross, Mercy Corps, to name a few.

Humanistic hope notwithstanding, when we face conditions so complex and overwhelming, it is easy to despair of the small difference any one person can make. On the other hand, thanks to recent discoveries in quantum physics, we know now, more than ever before, that everything is hitched to everything else. The consequence of this is that every little and big thing *does* make a difference, like the proverbial pebble in the pond.

In his much-lauded study of that moment when an idea, trend, or social behavior crosses a threshold and becomes a "tipping point," Malcolm Gladwell points out that this is often due to little causes having big effects, and the way contagiousness in one person can spark changes in another. What underlies progress "is a bedrock belief that change is possible, that people can radically transform their behavior or beliefs in the face of the right kind of impetus."[142] This is indeed good news.

Yet for all that is possible by human effort, my own view is that we would be sunk without "a divinity that shapes our ends, rough hew them as we will" (Shakespeare, *Hamlet*). Were this not so, our marks in time would be greatly diminished.

# 29.   HOPE AND HISTORY

*Causes and effects assume history marches forward, but history is not an army. It is a crab scuttling sideways, a drop of soft water wearing away a stone, an earthquake breaking centuries of tensions.*[143]

When we reflect on the merits of placing hope in human beings, we are making an assessment of the life of our species. Can we hope within human history, or do we have to project beyond it, to some other time and place?

History is the record of our strivings (be they written, spoken, artistically or visually represented), our accomplishments, our shortcomings, and the seminal events in our collective life. It is far more than dates and statistics; it is a primary means of ascertaining—at least in broad brushstrokes—the trajectory of our life together, within the context of a stupendous universe that is dynamically alive. Writing history is, on one hand, a kind of score keeping, not only of the successes and failures of governments and nations, but also of social movements, communities, and the powerful influence of individuals.

It matters greatly who writes history and how it is told or remembered. As women, minority people, and communities of color keep saying, history has often been written by the victors, that is, those in power, and there is considerable rewriting to do.

Often history is told through conflicts—a most unflattering perspective. As mentioned in the prologue, of approximately 3,500 years of human history, 3,144 of them have been years of war; and the remaining have been years of preparing for war or recovering from war. What a legacy! Thankfully, history can be read in other ways than by its conflicts, or, for that matter, by politics. For "what is popularly called politics is only a tiny part of what causes history to move."[144]

Here is another perspective: eminent historian Arnold Toynbee proposed that we read history through our responses to daunting challenges. It has been called the "challenge-response theory." Toynbee points out that our first instinct in the face of necessary changes has, more often than not, been resistance. We have often been reluctant responders who would not have made the various changes required of us without a crisis that forced the issue. For example, when it became necessary for our hunter-gatherer ancestors to settle down in one place, no one wanted to do so. But eventually they did because life demanded it. Our history has been a product of tension and stress as much as it has been a clear, linear drive.

Each generation is entrusted with its own unique time and circumstances. Our future very much depends upon whether we can respond to the enormous challenges besetting us, particularly the environmental crisis, the racism that perpetuates injustice, and the great imbalances that give rise to war, terrorism, disease, and the like.

In many ways human beings *have* responded to challenges with stupendous creativity. Let's consider a few responses from the realm of medicine toward diseases and health crises: the polio vaccine, motorized wheelchairs, malaria and smallpox vaccines, kidney dialysis, open heart surgery, organ transplants, artificial insemination. Or inventions that made life easier, especially in the areas of transportation and communication: electricity, the railroad, automobile, airplane, space shuttle, computer, telephone, e-mail, iPod. What a different sense of history we would have if we highlighted our proud communal achievements: the civil rights movement, the GI Bill, the Marshall Plan, or the loving, caring, healing, tending activities people have always engaged in, the world over. What if we told time by chronicling the efforts of those who have stood up to evil rather than memorizing the dates of wars?

When I despair of hoping in history and humankind, I am reminded that a number of African American leaders point to their history, and the communal survival of their people, as a source of hope. Charlayne Hunter-Gault, the television journalist, put it this way:

It's our history that has always been our source of hope . . . from the words of "Lift Every Voice and Sing" that reminded us that we've been brought out of the dark past and that the present is teaching us hope. Our history [speaks] of survival and prosperity in the face of societally engineered obstacles. . . ."[145]

She was only nineteen when she and fellow student Hamilton Holmes integrated the University of Georgia. What was the source of their courage?

It was based on the confidence that we had in what we had been given 100 percent by black people. It was the confidence, their insistence that although they didn't have the power to give us first-class citizenship, they had the power to give us a first-class sense of ourselves.[146]

The same could be said about the survival of marginalized people the world over who have endured despite suffering the cruelties of history. As was the case for African Americans, so too for every wave of immigrants to our shores: Somali, Eritreans, Poles, Czechs, Hmong, Rwandans, Haitians, Hispanics, Latinos, Jews, Palestinians, and numerous others. Whole governments conspired against them. It is a wonder that so many people not only survive but thrive against the odds—a true source of hope.

It may buoy hope to remember that history tends to zigzag. Progress in one era is disassembled in another. It is worth noting that civil rights acts had actually been passed in this country as early as 1866, 1870, and 1875. In 1865, the Thirteenth Amendment outlawed slavery throughout the United States. The Civil Rights Act of 1866 actually gave black men, including former slaves, legal rights to enforce contracts, own property, sue in court, and have legal protection for themselves and their property. But all that progress slid back downhill when, in 1883, the Supreme Court overturned the Civil Rights Act of 1875. Then, in 1896, it ruled again that "separate but equal" was legal. By 1900, all southern states had segregated schools and laws separating blacks from whites, and laws were passed preventing black citizens from voting—including new poll taxes, literacy requirements, and property qualifications.

To see the course of history as a back-and-forth process is not to excuse the inexcusable. To wake up to the ways in which we have perpetuated patterns of racism and injustice is to become aware of mind-numbing, despicable gaps between white culture and people of color. It makes you sit down and cry, in utter shame and disbelief. This level of anguish can be the impetus for us to turn to God.

# 30. HOPE AND GOD

*Only in the measure that we fail to yield completely into the mercy of God, will hope fail us. If we are willing to take it all the way, it will take us all the way.*[147]

For much of my life, I associated God with ideals: the good, the holy, perfection, compassion. In the long years of coping with illness, however, many of those ideals flew out the window. It's not that I no longer think of the divine as the All-Good or the Holy, but I realize ever more clearly that we human beings are often off balance in some way or another, and if God is to be found anywhere, it is in the messes, the chaos, and our attempts to partner with that force of goodness that brings forth the best in us. In fact, the uglier the situation, the more we need an undergirding of support.

While we human beings are capable of wondrous things, I side with those who believe the ultimate locus of hope is in God and God alone. Hope is being able to lean on God. In saying this, I do not mean that we are mere puppets or passive spectators, quite the contrary. Hope is a dimension of the divine that we share in, and it calls us to participate in the healing of the world. We have a crucial part to play, but we are not alone in running the show. Our intelligence, creativity, and conscience reflect an intelligence and a creative power much vaster than what we can lay claim to by ourselves. This is theistic hope, of which there are healthy and unhealthy varieties.

If we were honest about it, even those of us who claim a spiritual life and reliance on God might well prefer to lean elsewhere, if we could. On ourselves, for instance, on our gifts and talents, on our intelligence and imagination, on our social networks. Yet when any of these sources falter, hope also begins to quiver and we realize that "our" health, "our" resources, "our" friends are not possessions we can own or control, but gifts we have received. And all of them, materially speaking, can be lost; in fact, they will be lost to us one day.

I must admit to being guilty myself of what Parker Palmer calls "functional atheism," paying lip service through my language to God, but by my actions assuming that God does not exist or is sleeping and not all that interested in lending aid.[148] I know I am not alone in this. It is reported that three quarters of Americans believe the Bible says God helps those who help themselves—a testament to the stock we place in our can-do, take-charge mode of living.

Our power, beauty, and capacity for intimacy with God notwithstanding, humanism is not enough to explain us. Neither our intelligence, imagination, nor creative genius can be understood apart from the context in which we live and die—a universe fourteen billion years in the making, and still being created. We are the offspring of this stupendous creative force.

One of the things any recovering addict will tell you is that sobriety depends upon a "higher power," however that power be conceived. Many in recovery say there is no earthly way she could have charted her own course to such a vastly changed life. Reflecting on her path through addiction, the quick-witted and quirky Anne Lamott says of grace that it is "unearned love . . . the help you receive when you have no bright ideas left, when you are empty and desperate and have discovered that your best thinking and most charming charm have failed you."[149]

You don't have to be an addict to be reminded that it's not all up to you. God, it seems, cannot reach the self-reliant. This is why it can take considerable hollowing out before we have enough space within to receive that which we did not generate. When we give up our striving, cease trying to fill the emptiness ourselves, and "stand in the dark, there finally may be a place in us to be filled with light other than our own, and by it, come to know that there is neither the need to run nor the possibility of hiding. It is in this emptiness and stillness . . . that hope begins."[150]

It is only when we have ceased to anchor hope in getting all we want materially, and in having the externals all line up in our favor, that we are ready for the awareness that hope, biblically speaking, is never equated with the status quo. It is based on something more abiding than material conditions. This is why "hope is still there when all your worst fears have been realized."[151]

Mystic Julian of Norwich's conviction that "all shall be well, and all shall be well, and all manner of things shall be well" is a theological position. It was not a summation she came to by looking around at the social situation in fourteenth-century England, but from a gut-level conviction that this is God's world, and that, ultimately, we cannot be lost to God because our universe and our little human lives are held in the great curvature of love. God's creative purposes will come to be. In the meanwhile, it is strengthening to remember that there is nowhere to go where God is not. As the psalmist said:

God is our refuge and strength,
a very present help in trouble.
Therefore we will not fear, though the earth should change,
though the mountains shake in the heart of the sea;
though its waters roar and foam,
though the mountains tremble with its tumult. (Psalm 46:1-3)

Those who understand the universe through both scientific and theological lenses might translate the biblical poet's reassurance in these terms: come what may in the human realm, the sun and moon will still continue to revolve in their courses, the sea will keep undulating in its timeless rhythms, and life's large universal patterns, let loose in a gigantic cosmos, will keep unfolding. Lest we romanticize this idea, however, many would remind us that cataclysm is one of the powers in the universe that reoccurs. Some say we are in the fifth or sixth period of cataclysm in the life of earth. But that is another story.

Theistic hope is a worldview that enlists our participation in the work of *tikkun olam*, that beautiful and encompassing Hebrew term that means "healing the tear in the fabric of creation," the work we were born for. God is the source of this vision and of the grace and grit to help us partner in its accomplishment. But we are a part of the equation. Sometimes it is difficult to believe our Partner is there. Surely God feels the same about us. Etty Hillesum, writing in her journal from Auschwitz, captures the irony that there are ways in which God may have need of us:

One thing is becoming increasingly clear to me: that You cannot help us, that we must help You to help ourselves. And that is all we can manage these days, and all that really matters: that we safeguard that little piece of You, God, in ourselves. And perhaps in others as well . . . we must help You and defend Your dwelling place inside us to the last. [152]

How different this is from a theistic optimism that sees the inevitable ending all sewn up in the second coming of Christ, say, or a new messianic age. In this mostly passive posture, little is required of us, in the meantime, beyond holding tightly to particular beliefs. In other words: don't worry, be happy, in a matter of time, when God is good and ready, the end times will arrive.

There is another kind of theistic hope, one that is not directly related quid pro quo to the external situation. It is a kind of hope that I cannot quite imagine, though I have heard of it. My mentor, Gerald May at the Shalem Institute for Spiritual Formation, tells of a trip he took to the war-torn Baltic region some years ago, and the people he met whose hope was still standing, even after complete devastation. There, he experienced a transformed hope "in people who have suffered more than anyone deserves." When he saw this hope, he "was blinded by it."

> In the summer of 1994, I joined a small pilgrimage to Bosnia. I had the opportunity to speak with poor people who had lost everything: houses, possessions, entire families. As they told us their stories through tears of grief, I sensed deep hope in them. Through interpreters I asked if it were true. "Yes, hope," they smiled. I asked if it was hope for peace. "No, things have gone too far for that." I asked if they hoped the United Nations or the United States would intervene in some positive way. "No, it's too late for that." I asked them, "Then, what is it you are hoping for?" They were silent. They could not think of a thing to hope for, yet there it was, undeniable hope shining in them. I asked one last question. "How can you hope, when there's nothing to hope for?" The answer was, "Bog," the Serbo-Croatian word for God.
>
> Thus I have had some glimpses into the nature of this transformed hope. I believe I have experienced moments of it myself, but I can neither fathom nor comprehend it. Like contemplative faith and love, it evades my understanding. The one thing I can say positively about these transformed qualities is that to discover them, in oneself or in another, brings the deepest reassurance I have ever experienced.[153]

If there is that of God in us, there is hope for us. Which brings us to the subject of the divine/human relationship.

# 31.

# HOPE AS PARTNERSHIP
# BETWEEN HUMAN AND DIVINE

*We must try to love so well the world, that we may believe, in the end, in God.*

—Robert Penn Warren

*At the macro level hope does not have to do with our private agendas, but it does have to do with moving us toward where it is going. Ultimately, hope is divine energy and intelligence moving toward the accomplishment of its purposes; it makes use of us, rather than we of it.*[154]

Whether you believe hope is a gift from an infinite source, or an inherent human quality (one that we exercise and can strengthen over time), human beings simply are bound up with the divine in an alchemy whose exact proportions we can never fully know. Another way to think about the source of hope is to speak of human and divine energies intermingling in the work of doing good in the world. Hope lives in two kinds of partnerships: those between people, and those between people and God. Since we have already given considerable attention to human-to-human partnerships, I want to focus here on our partnership with God.

## HUMAN PARTNERSHIPS

When I think of people who are deeply humane, that is, compassionate, kind, and attentive to others' needs, they do not fit the dramatic role of hero. They simply put their hands to the plow in the steady, day-by-day work of raising children or grandchildren, tending to elderly parents, driving their friends to chemotherapy, volunteering in their community, contributing by means of checkbook justice, or living with a host of challenges without being dominated by them.

Some people lean intentionally on God along the way. Others do not. In either case, something Jesus purportedly said to his friends is relevant here. According to the Gospel writer, he said that the kingdom of God (or rule of God) is *between* you and *among* you (Luke 17:21). I take this to mean our exchanges with each other have the potential to become alive with the dynamism of mercy and love. It is there, in our actions more than in words or beliefs, that the divine presence is ignited. In other words, human relationships are like electrical wires. Whether it is a quiet current they carry or the high-voltage variety, they carry the presence of God into the world when they have at their heart kindness, compassion, generosity. Hope lives wherever people act out of their best selves.

Hope is to be found in the steadfastness of those who care for others: in Alzheimer's units, homeless shelters, daycare centers, schools, prisons, treatment centers, food pantries, as well as in peace efforts, efforts to eliminate poverty, racism, and fear. It is to be found when people do the right thing, regardless of its effects. Think foster families who take in children who have been profoundly traumatized and require extraordinary patience and care. Or people staging protests against government policies that further injure the vulnerable. If we were as conscious of this aspect of human behavior as we were of our flaws, we could celebrate all that is right with the world, even now.

## COUNTERING BAD NEWS WITH REASONS TO CELEBRATE

While we are focusing on the best in us, let me note that behind every newspaper article conveying bad news are stories filled with good news that never gets reported. Behind every headline about war, many hands are at work for peace. Behind every story of revenge, there are countless others finding forgiveness. Behind the stories of greed are people seeking equality or giving something valuable away. I notice in today's *Seattle Times* that seven small dams in the state of Washington are being dismantled, and the salmon are returning to spawn in these rivers again. Just next to it is an article about the three thousandth American military person to be killed in Iraq. Oh, and here, in the Minneapolis *Star Tribune*, is a story about a small flower shop that was burned to the ground by arson. Within a week, the owners had been given the use of a large truck as a makeshift store, and hundreds of people lined up, buying and placing orders for six thousand roses to help the owners return to business.

# Religious Motivation at Its Best

At the Holocaust Museum in Washington, D.C., there is a memorial that honors the courageous few who came to the aid of Jews and others who were swept up in the evil unleashed by the Nazi killers in the Second World War. It is a literal wall called "The Rescuers Wall." In some places, communities and organizations are named in dark letters on the stark white wall. In other places, individuals are noted. Among them is a small photograph of a Protestant clergyman named André Trocmé, his wife, Magda, and their four children. They, along with the relatively poor villagers of Le Chambon-sur-Lignon and its surrounding farms (including Catholics, other Protestants, and nonreligious people), stood up to evil at great risk to themselves. Descendants of French Huguenots who had been persecuted themselves, Trocmé's congregation, in quiet partnership with their neighbors, stepped into the biblical demands to resist evil, harboring nearly five thousand Jewish children in the shadow of the Third Reich. During those haunted years, these people of humble means fed and clothed others' children, led them in song and dance, educated them in one or another of the villages' schools, and hid them, saving their lives by doing so.[155]

Six decades later, conflicts still rage across the globe; in many cases, the roots of controversy and struggle are to be found in racial and religious differences. This being the case, if there is hope for our ethnically and religiously divided world, it is in the capacity of some people to treat others as themselves, and to see themselves as their brothers' and sisters' keepers, regardless of the others' religious persuasion. Whether the motivation for such action is people's sheer goodness or the ethical imperatives of a religious tradition, it is actions that matter. While it is true that religion can become a tremendous force of evil, it can also be a tremendous force for good. Nothing seems to make us more dangerous than religion wrongly used. Yet nothing makes us kinder.

## The Intermingling of the Human and the Divine

The second partnership is that between people and God. I believe we are encoded from birth with "that of God in us," as the Quakers are wont to say. This encoding calls us beyond ourselves to lives of meaning, purpose, authenticity, and community. Some have named this the "higher self" (e.g., the psychosynthesis school of transpersonal psychology). Others call it the "inner being" (St. Paul, for example, in his letter to the Ephesians, 3:16). By whatever name we call this impulse, it lies at the base of civility and citizenship. This best-in-us does not garner nearly enough attention, and this omission shortchanges us. Just as we need to be awake to hideous injustices, we also need to see reflected back to us those ways in which a majority of earth's people are involved, day to day, year by year, in the well-being of others. This sacred instinct is as much at the heart of what keeps history moving as our baser motivations, like fear and greed.

I return to Etty Hillesum again, as an example of a person living out of her highest self and in conscious awareness of the divine, even in the most despicable of circumstances. Her outlook on the decimation of European Jews bears dramatic testimony not only to the buoyancy and radiance of the human spirit, but to the need for divine/human partnership. Even from inside the walls of a death camp, she was able to say:

> I often see visions of poisonous green smoke; I am with the hungry and with the ill-treated and dying every day, but I am also with the jasmine and with that piece of sky beyond my window. If God does not help me to go on, then I shall have to help God. . . . I'll just take all the faces and familiar gestures I have collected and hang them up along the walls of my inner space so that they will always be with me. . . . There is no hidden poet in me, just a little piece of God that might grow into poetry . . . and a camp needs a poet . . . one who experiences life there, even there, as a bard, and is able to sing about it. . . . Let me be the thinking heart of these barracks. . . . For every prison needs a poet.[156]

The understanding that divine agency and human agency are bound together is not merely one aspect of Jewish biblical history; it is *the* defining story. After years of slavery in Egypt, the ancient Jews stumbled through the wilderness, pursued by their captors, until they were driven to the edge of the Red Sea. They were, understandably, terrified. So they did what many of us seem to do in a crisis—blame someone else. In this case, they blamed Moses. "Was it because there were no graves in Egypt that you have taken us away to die in the wilderness? . . . For it would have been better for us to serve the Egyptians than to die in the wilderness" (Exodus 14:11-12).

Pretty soon Moses had had enough of their complaining, so he started in on God. Which in turn angered God—according to the writer(s) of the book of Exodus. "Why do you cry out to me?" asks God, of Moses. "Tell the Israelites to go forward" (Exodus 14:15). Hmmm. Now there's a concept bound to frighten many. The people learned, to their dismay, that they would have to participate in their own exodus. They had to step in the direction that seemed to lead toward freedom, even though it appeared that they might drown in the process. God said: "Go forward." They would have to move, step by soggy, desperate step, through the waters of the Red Sea. They would not be ferried around it, nor helicoptered above it, nor magically saved from making the passage. This line would come in handy for leaders in a variety of settings: "Stop complaining, you dolts, and take the next step already!" Which brings us once again to the participatory nature of hope.

It has often been my experience that the waters do not part until I take the risk of stepping into them. Yet once I take the risk of acting on behalf of my deepest inclinations, I have the sense of being undergirded by a power beyond my own. Let me hasten to add that it does not always feel this way in the middle of stepping forward. It can be only in retrospect that I see this comingling of energies, human and divine.

> Until one is committed there is hesitancy, the chance to draw back . . . the moment one definitely commits oneself, then providence moves too. All sorts of things occur to help one that would never otherwise have occurred. A whole stream of events issues from the decision, raising in one's favour all manner of unforeseen incidents and meetings and material assistance which no man could have dreamt would have come his way. I have learned a deep respect for one of Goethe's couplets: "Whatever you can do, or dream you can, begin it. Boldness has genius, power and magic in it."[157]

## THE TRADITION OF BLESSING

There is a tradition in Judaism that ritualizes the intermingling of human and divine. It is the practice of blessings. A blessing is a short, meditative exercise in which a person focuses on the goodness of something in such a way that it creates an opening for God. In fact, the gratitude that is at the heart of a blessing keeps a person awake to the divine presence. There are blessings for just about everything. There is the blessing for seeing a sunrise, for seeing a sunset, for the gift of food, for meeting an old friend, for embarking on a journey, and for a safe return.

> Jewish tradition teaches that the simple action of a brakha (blessing) has a cosmic affect, for a brakha causes shefa, the "abundant flow" of God's love and goodness, to pour into the world. Like a hand on the faucet, each brakha turns on the tap. . . . A brakha completes our energy exchange with God. We are partners in a sacred cycle of giving and receiving in which we are not only "on the take." When we offer our blessings, we raise up sparks of holiness, releasing the God-light housed in our world back to its Source. We receivers become givers and the nurturing flow is sustained.[158]

The practice of seeing goodness in the everyday and the work of justice both draw God's presence into the world.

# 32. HOPE'S ORIGINS IN MYSTERY

*Hope is a strange invention—Of this electric Adjunct*
*A Patent of the Heart—Not anything is known*
*In unremitting action But its unique momentum*
*Yet never wearing out—Embellish all we own*[159]

*Hope resides in the dark, in the essential unknowability*
*of the world.*[160]

Having spent all these chapters exploring the nature of hope, I trust we can agree that it is a multilayered subject and that many of hope's attributes can be studied and understood. I assume you and I would object to Emily Dickinson's description of hope as an "adjunct," some add-on that is not essentially a part of life. On the contrary, hope is at the core of every life. Even so, there are mysteries surrounding hope that will remain mysteries. Here is one of them: at times hope does not even take an object; it is simply there, a silent partner come alongside to accompany us. Hope helps us lean with some measure of confidence into the future.

There are times when hope is not distilled enough to be a clear emotion, nor so faint that we cannot see its signature. Yet if we had words to explain it, we might say that hope's stirrings in a life seemed more real and more trustworthy than any material dimension of reality. I am thinking here of those rare (night) dreams that seem to have been sent to us as pure gifts meant to lift our spirits. They came at just the time we needed them most, or they left an imprint that gave us the courage to expect goodness in the days or weeks to come. I also think of subtle stirrings of spirit that I have experienced, which elude every attempt to describe or explain them. I think of them as "visitations." They arrived when I was at my absolute lowest, bringing hope and reassurance.

One of the essential aspects of hope that remains veiled in mystery is its origins. I am not talking here about the hopes that can be attributed to positive outcomes in the external world, but to the hope that is present even when the external situation is grim and there is no rational reason to hope whatsoever. In such circumstances a person wonders, where does hope begin?

I referred earlier to a pristine mountain lake in northern Idaho where my family has a summer cabin, and to the fact that in some places the lake bottom has never been found. Divers have tried to find it on a number of occasions, including a time forty years ago when four teenagers drowned in a late-night boating accident. However, in its deepest places, Hayden Lake merges with an underground aquifer, leaving the bottom inaccessible.

In just the same way, it can be hard to tell when hope is a divine gift that originates somewhere else and when it is an inherent quality of human character. A spark of hope can be ignited by a relationship between one person and another, between a person and a community. It can also be enkindled by a person's relationship with God or the natural world. Still we might ask, where does hope come from?

In closing, I would like to linger for a moment on the idea that hope originates from somewhere beyond us and to illustrate this concept by drawing on the reflections of Vaclav Havel, during the nearly five years he spent in prison. He writes:

> I think that the deepest and most important form of hope, the only one that can keep us above water and urge us to good works, and the only true source of the breathtaking dimension of the human spirit and its efforts, is something we get, as if were from "elsewhere." Hope is a state of mind, not of the world.[161]

It is a good thing we cannot get to the bottom of hope. This keeps its otherness alive and prevents our taking it for granted. It underscores hope's multifaceted nature and the limits of human understanding. Who can say, after all, why one person is able to access hope in a trying situation and another person has to work and pray and fight like mad just to stay in hope's vicinity? Who can say why hope is generally present in children, no matter their circumstances? There are wellsprings of hope not accessible to reason, nor pried open by will.

Having been called upon as a minister to offer consoling, hopeful words in difficult situations—beside hospital beds, at funerals, and while standing with grieving families at a loved one's grave—I share Emily Dickinson's humility about our ever being able to completely understand hope, especially how it can return after it has been lost, and why it can remain elusive, even for those who have done everything they know to do to get in position to receive hope again.

Whatever its sources, I wholeheartedly agree with Dickinson that hope's presence "embellishes all we own." This essence, this intelligence, this energy, this presence we call hope enlivens every project and adds luster and energy to every circumstance it graces. It is the vocation of those of us who are blessed with a fair measure of hope to keep bringing it to bear on the darkness of our time. Surely it is not just we who are in search of hope, but hope is also in search of us. Hope "has to do with moving us toward where it is going. Ultimately, hope is divine energy and intelligence moving toward the accomplishment of its purposes; it makes use of us, rather than we of it."[162]

# A Concluding Personal Word

A s I close these reflections, I am able to say that the one overriding personal hope, from which I began these reflections—the hope for robust, dependable health—has been met in significant ways. Thanks to many healers and a whole regimen of aids, I can now claim steadier health than I could at any time in the past ten years. For this I am deeply grateful. Even so, this is an ongoing balancing act, and the old symptoms are never far away.

One of the outcomes of my apprenticeship to hope is that I can no longer embrace hope for my own well-being without also embracing hopes for the larger human family. The personal and the communal are truly one.

# QUESTIONS FOR REFLECTION AND DISCUSSION

## 1. THE NATURE OF HOPE

1. Do you consider yourself a hopeful person? If so, what factors contribute to this? If not, what factors contribute to your not being a particularly hopeful person?

2. What life circumstances have most threatened your hope?

3. Would you agree with writer Barbara Kingsolver that hope is a "basic instinct, baser even than hate"?

## 2. HOPE DIFFERS FROM OPTIMISM

1. Think about people you know who have an optimistic attitude about most things. What are the gifts and benefits of optimism?

2. Can you name examples of optimism that rode roughshod over the facts of the situation and skirted around the truth in such a way that genuine hope was crowded out?

3. It has been said that Ronald Reagan was our most optimistic president. When is optimism a virtue in a leader? When might it be a hindrance?

## 3. LIVING WITH A BEAST

1. Most of us have had to contend with one sort of "beast" or another. What is/ are yours? What do you know from contending with it about the ways hope can be threatened, even lost, and, if one is fortunate, found again?

2. What does the fact that hope can be lost and found say about the nature of hope?

3. What do you know about coping strategies and the work it can take just to stay in hope's vicinity?

## 4. Hope's Limits

1. William Lynch says that not all things can be hoped for. How is it both helpful and healthy to acknowledge that hope is not absolute in its range? Think of situations on both a personal level and a societal level where this is true.

2. Can you imagine a circumstance in which an overly idealistic outlook on some matter actually diminished hope?

3. How might a person come to embrace hope's (life's) limits when she or he is more naturally inclined to resist the idea of limits?

## 5. Hope and Imagination

1. Have you been a witness to the power of the human imagination and the way it can come up with solutions to problems, expand one's worldview, and enable a person to live with a difficult present? Explain.

2. Where might one look for examples of the communal imagination?

3. Where is imagination needed most if our species is to have a future and if our planet is to be healthy? In other words, what challenges need our best thinking, creativity, and imagination?

## 6. Help — Hope's Companion

1. What are our culture's attitudes toward giving and receiving help?

2. It can be difficult to ask for and/or receive help. What attitudes and dynamics between giver and receiver make it easiest to receive? What kinds of giving diminish the receiver?

3. Have you ever declined help or chosen not to ask for it, forfeiting an opportunity to bolster hope in the process? Explain.

## 7. Our Heritage of Hope

1. When you think about your own family, would you say they transmitted hope to you? If so, how was it expressed? Did it come clothed in their attitudes toward difficulty? In their skills, tenacity, or worldview? Perhaps you had to develop hope *in spite of* your family. If so, how would you say this happened?

2. Where (and in whom) did you see resilience embodied in your formative years?

3. What challenges, external and internal, historical and personal, shaped the contours of hope in your parents' and grandparents' lives?

## 8. The Anchor — Symbol of Hope

1. What do you make of the anchor symbol as a metaphor for hope? Does it resonate for you? Why or why not?

2. What else might the early Christians have seen in this symbol?

3. In Buddhist teachings, suffering comes as a result of attachment to something, suggesting that letting go can be the better path. Yet perhaps the Buddhist idea of seeking refuge—in teachings, in community, in the story of Buddha—is akin to being anchored. What are your thoughts on this?

## 9. Borrowing Hope

1. Have you ever had to borrow hope? If so, what made the person who "held" hope for you trustworthy?

2. Has anyone borrowed hope from you? What was it like to be on that end of the continuum?

3. What are examples of hope being borrowed on a communal level?

## 10. Hope as a Choice

1. What do you think of the suggestion that a person (who may be a patient in a hospital or health care setting) has the right to choose hope?

2. If people in the medical world respected this right, would it make a difference in their relationships with, and attitude toward, those with serious illness? If so, how?

3. Have you ever witnessed hope in another that was more a life stance than a reflection of external circumstances? If so, explain.

## 11. Mature Hope

1. What qualities or characteristics do you associate with mature hope? With immature hope?

2. What factors contribute to the development of mature hope?

3. Have you seen—either in yourself or in another—the embodiment of a kind of hope that "does not come at the end, as the feeling that results from a happy outcome," but something that "lies at the beginning, as a pulse of truth that it sends forth"?[163] If so, what contributes to this kind of hope?

## 12. Relapse and Its Emotional Fallout

1. What do you know about yourself in relation to disappointment, to losing ground after attaining some goal or realizing a particular hope? Have you had the experience of hope dwindling, not so much because of any one factor, but because of the "too-muchness" or "too-longness" of something?

2. What advice would you give another person who is contending with some kind of relapse/severe discouragement?

3. What strategies might one use to stay connected to hope when there seems to be no light at the end of the tunnel?

## 13. OTHER THREATS TO HOPE

1. What do you know about yourself and the ways in which you lose hope from time to time? Are there patterns to this?

2. What do you know from personal experience, or from watching others, about how hope is found again?

3. Even if a person can't simply go out and find hope, are there ways in which to get in position to receive it? Are there inward postures or attitudes that help it return? Explain.

## 14. SPIRITUAL FALLOUT: ILLNESS "CAN RUIN YOUR MANNERS TOWARD GOD"

1. If you are someone who believes in God, have you been in situations that have challenged your faith in God? If so, what aspects of divinity no longer seemed accurate in the face of that challenge?

2. If you are not someone who believes in God, you have probably met up with something that challenged your worldview, maybe threatening it altogether, ripping right into the way you made sense of the world, undermining the meanings that held you up. What has threatened you in such a total way?

3. If you are a person of faith, what has most challenged your faith? What has most strengthened it? Would you say that the challenges have, over time, made your faith stronger and more mature?

## 15. FALSE HOPE

1. Scan the advertisements in a newspaper or magazine or online. Distinguish the promises claimed that might in fact be true from those that constitute out-and-out false hope.

2. What are some of the idealizations in our culture that border on false hope?

3. Have you ever taken the bait on a promise that turned out to be false? What impact did this have on your hope and your ways of reaching toward it?

## 16. Provisional Hope

1. Provisional hope has its place. It can be a leaning place, strong enough to get you through, even if it is not a permanent solution. What forms of provisional hope have you experienced?

2. Are there examples from your community's life of provisional hope?

3. What political, environmental, or physical crises in the world call for provisional hope at the very least, and what might this hope "look like"?

## 17. Finding Meaning Trumps Particular Outcomes

1. How has hope contributed to your understanding of the meaning of difficult, troubling, or even tragic events?

2. In what ways might hope encourage and enable you to take meaningful action?

3. How do you understand the relationship between hope and vision and imagination?

## 18. Hope Seeks the Bigger Picture

1. When you feel pressed down by life's challenges, what are the ways in which you try to seek a larger view?

2. Can you think of ways in which you've been able to reframe a situation? When have you seen this capacity in another person?

3. What is the "larger context" within which you see and experience your life?

## 19. Hope's Relationship to Faith

1. How do you think of faith? How would you distinguish it from hope?

2. Do you think these distinctions matter? Why or why not?

3. Is it helpful to think of faith as something that goes far beyond belief? Why or why not?

## 20. Hope and Truth Sit Side by Side

1. Think of examples in which authentic hope was compromised because it was not in conversation with truth.

2. How might a person be in conversation with truth *and* choose to hope? How might these paradoxes be embraced?

3. In what ways might truth challenge hope? In what ways might hope open one to the truth?


## 21. When Hope Takes Work

1. Would you agree with Emily Dickinson, who says of hope, "Never, in Extremity, It asked a crumb of Me"?

2. Recall a time in which it took work for you to stay in hope's vicinity. How did you cope? What attitudes, actions, or mind-sets were helpful?

3. Have you ever experienced yourself in "limbo"? Explain. What did you do?


## 22. Detecting Patterns — A Cause for Hope

1. For the author, realizing that certain choices and actions had consequences was a cause for hope, because it meant the symptoms of her illness were not completely random. There were patterns to it. How might this realization help in addressing difficult situations?

2. Have you ever experienced what the author calls a "bargainer's hope"?

3. What do you know from your own experience of coming back to hope about the road back?


## 23. How Hope Returns

1. What is your own experience of how hope returns?

2. While it's not possible to go out and get hope exactly, there may be certain places we can go, certain things we can do that can get us in position to receive

hope, at least. What are some of the tried and true ways you become available to hope? Is it being with certain people? Listening to particular music? Going out to your garden? Finding your prayer corner, your favorite writer, a beloved place in the woods? Explain.

3. What are some of the surprising ways hope returns?

## 24. Sheltering Hope

1. In what ways have you experienced the vulnerability of hope?

2. Have you ever had to "shelter hope"? What did you do?

3. When hope's goal seems elusive, what do you do to nourish hope?

## 25. Stories Can Be Medicine

1. Do you see yourself as part of a larger story? If so, what story or stories? How have you ever found yourself within the lines of a story, be it a mythic story, a biblical story, a fictional story, a cultural story, or a religious story, that helped you make sense of things and served to orient you?

2. Is there a story that has provided solace? If so, what is it?

3. Is there a story that has enabled you to endure something you might not have been able to endure without it? Explain.

## 26. In Praise of Coping

1. Sometimes life is an endurance contest. It's a matter of coping, a necessary action, even if it is a far cry from thriving. What is your own experience of the need to draw on every possible resource to get through a particular time?

2. What is the place of anger in such situations?

3. Where can hope be found in coping, even if it doesn't look like hope?

## 27. Surprising Sources of Hope

1. What are some of the sources of your own hope that came from unexpected places?

2. Remember the story of Etty Hillesum. What small, ordinary things keep your spirit alive in difficult times?

3. Read through a newspaper or magazine; what surprising hopes do you discover? What do these surprises do to your own sense of hope?


## 28. Humanistic Hope

1. Name or list as many people as you can who embody humanistic hope, anchoring them in examples. In other words, what attributes or actions make these people such inspiring examples of the best in our species? (Include those you know personally who are otherwise unknown outside your circle.)

2. Do any of these hopeful people exhibit what St. Augustine called hope's children—anger and courage? Anger at the way things are and the courage to make sure they do not remain as they are?

3. When you think of a particular challenge that we face in the world, be it poverty, hunger, or resorting to war to solve our problems, what values/attributes and actions are most needed to address them?


## 29. Hope and History

1. What is your own view of human history? Do you think we are evolving in a positive way? Are there places to look in history that demonstrate this? Or are you less than sanguine about it, given our propensities? What examples would you draw on to support either view?

2. When you think of the world's people, who among us may have least cause for hope, given what has happened to them over time? Which people have most cause for hope, at least in terms of their material well-being?

3. Given your own talents, skills, training, temperament, and the realities about our world that trouble you most, how would you characterize this time in history? What is needed most? How or what do you need to contribute?

## 30. Hope and God

1. Do you know people—perhaps this includes yourself—who have gotten free of addiction, who attribute some measure of their sobriety to a higher power?

2. What is your own view of the divine?

3. Have you ever looked back at your life and wondered how you made it? Would you ascribe this to the grace of God? Explain.

## 31. Hope as Partnership between Human and Divine

1. Have you ever felt as though your own human actions were strengthened by a power beyond your own? If so, talk about this. If not, talk about that.

2. Can you relate to still having hope even when all your worst fears have been realized?

3. Are there ways certain religious people talk about the divine/human relationship that do not sit right with you? Explain.

## 32. Hope's Origins in Mystery

1. While we know a great deal about hope's power to sustain and embellish, it's source(s) remains mysterious. Where would you locate hope's origins?

2. Have you ever experienced objectless hope, hope without a specific goal? If so, describe the feeling. If not, can you imagine such hope?

3. In what ways does hope help you "lean with some measure of confidence into the future"?

# NOTES

1. Emily Dickinson, *Final Harvest: Poems*, ed. Thomas H. Johnson (New York: Back Bay Books, 1964), 34–35.

2. Lynne Olson, *Freedom's Daughters: The Unsung Heroines of the Civil Rights Movement from 1830 to 1970* (New York: Scribner, 2001), 254.

3. Barbara Kingsolver, *Small Wonder: Essays* (New York: Harper Perennial, 2003), 21.

4. Vaclav Havel, *Letters to Olga* (New York: Henry Holt and Company, 1983), 53.

5. Charles Olson, "The Days," in *Teaching with Fire*, ed. Sam M. Intrator and Megan Scribner (San Francisco: Jossey-Bass, 2003), 117.

6. Kingsolver, *Small Wonder*, 21.

7. Barbara Kingsolver, *High Tide in Tucson: Essays from Now or Never* (New York: Harper Perennial, 1996), 16.

8. Rebecca Solnit, *Hope in the Dark: Untold Histories, Wild Possibilities* (New York: Nation Books, 2004), 5.

9. Scott Russell Sanders, *Hunting for Hope: A Father's Journeys* (Boston: Beacon, 1998), 19.

10. Jerome Groopman, *The Anatomy of Hope: How People Prevail in the Face of Illness* (New York: Random House, 2004), xiv.

11. Solnit, *Hope in the Dark*, 4.

12. Cynthia Bourgeault, *Mystical Hope: Trusting in the Mercy of God* (Lanham, Md.: Cowley, 2001), 86–87.

13. William Sloane Coffin, "The Greatest Hope," in *The Collected Sermons of William Sloane Coffin: The Riverside Years, Vol. 1* (Louisville: Westminster John Knox, 2008).

14. Roy Fairchild, *Finding Hope Again: A Guide to Counseling Depression* (New York: Harper & Row, 1980), 51.

15. Marge Piercy, *The Art of Blessing the Day: Poems with a Jewish Theme* (New York: Alfred Knopf, 1999), 4–5.

16. Groopman, *The Anatomy of Hope*, xiv.

17. Fairchild, *Finding Hope Again*, 50–51.

18. Sanders, *Hunting for Hope*, 19.

19. Yann Martel, *Life of Pi* (New York: Harcourt, 2001), 63.

20. Ibid., 273.

21. William Lynch, *Images of Hope: Imagination as Healer of the Hopeless* (Notre Dame: University of Notre Dame Press, 1974), 54–55.

22. Ibid., 61.

23. Nancy Mairs, *Waist-High in the World* (Boston: Beacon, 1996), 31.

24. Ibid., 81.

25. Lynch, *Images of Hope*, 23.

26. Samuel Taylor Coleridge, quoted in *Big Questions, Worthy Dreams*, by Sharon Daloz Parks (San Francisco: Jossey-Bass, 2000), 108.

27. Parks, *Big Questions, Worthy Dreams*, 20.

28. Ira Progoff, *At a Journal Workshop* (New York: Tarcher, 1975).

29. Jean-Dominique Bauby, *The Diving Bell and the Butterfly* (New York: Vintage, 1997), 20.

30. Ibid., 23.

31. Ibid., 25.

32. Terry Tempest Williams, *The Open Space of Democracy* (Great Barrington, Mass.: The Orion Society, 2004), 80.

33. Lynch, *Images of Hope*, 24.

34. Patricia Weaver Francisco, *Telling* (New York: Harper Collins, 1999), 2–3.

35. Ibid., 42.

36. Ibid., 42–43.

37. Mairs, *Waist-High in the World*, 71.

38. Ibid., 83–84.

39. From the song "We Are," on the album *Sacred Ground*, by Sweet Honey in the Rock, Earthbeat, 1995 (P.O. Box 1460, Redway, CA, 95560-1400).

40. Maggie Craddock, *The Authentic Career: Following the Path of Self-Discovery to Professional Fulfillment* (Novato, Calif.: New World Library, 2004), 64.

41. Sanders, *Hunting for Hope*, 7–10.

42. Ibid., 21.

43. "My Anchor Holds," lyrics by William Martin, music by Daniel Towner, 1902.

44. Julian of Norwich, *Showings*, trans. and ed. Edmund Colledge and James Walsh, SJ, Classics of Western Spirituality Series (Mahwah, N.J.: Paulist Press, 1978), 225.

45. Jean Houston, *Jump Time: Shaping Your Future in a World of Radical Change* (Boulder: Sentient Publications, 2004), 111.

46. Dickinson, *Final Harvest*, 166.

47. Richard B. Sewall, *The Life of Emily Dickinson* (Boston: Harvard University Press, 1980), 591.

48. Groopman, *The Anatomy of Hope*, 81.

49. Ibid., 164.

50. Bill Bradley, quoted in *Restoring Hope: Conversations on the Future of Black America*, by Cornel West (Boston: Beacon, 1999), 48.

51. Bourgeault, *Mystical Hope*, 78–79.

52. Lynch, *Images of Hope*, 36.

53. Susan Griffin, *What Her Body Thought: A Journey into the Shadows* (New York: HarperOne, 1999), 27.

54. Ibid.

55. Oliver Sacks, "A Surgeon's Life," in *Vintage Sacks* (New York: Vintage, 2004), 110.

56. Donald Hall, *The Best Day the Worst Day: Life with Jane Kenyon* (Boston: Mariner Books, 2006), 120.

57. Irving Greenberg, *For the Sake of Heaven and Earth: The Encounter between Judaism and Christianity* (Philadelphia: Jewish Publication Society, 2004), 163.

58. Viktor Frankl, *Man's Search for Meaning* (New York: Washington Square Press, 1984), 97.

59. Ibid.

60. Solnit, *Hope in the Dark*, 81–82.

61. Lynch, *Images of Hope*, 55.

62. Ibid., 106–7.

63. Ibid., 116.

64. Jane Kenyon, "Having It Out with Melancholy," in *Constance: Poems* (St. Paul: Graywolf, 1993), 21.

65. Jonathan Kozol, *Ordinary Resurrections: Children in the Years of Hope* (New York: Crown, 2000), 72.

66. Hall, *The Best Day the Worst Day*, 97.

67. Solnit, *Hope in the Dark*, 9.

68. Lynch, *Images of Hope*, 243.

69. Vaclav Havel, *Disturbing the Peace* (New York: Alfred A. Knopf, 1990), 181.

70. Ibid., 154.

71. Ibid., 181.

72. Havel, *Letters to Olga*, 150.

73. James Gertmenian, from a sermon, "All Shall Be Well," delivered December 5, 2004, Plymouth Congregational Church, Minneapolis.

74. Havel, *Letters to Olga*, 243.

75. Ibid., 242.

76. Lynch, *Images of Hope*, 36.

77. Abraham Joshua Heschel, *The Sabbath* (New York: Noonday, 1951) 83.

78. Solnit, *Hope in the Dark*, 55–56.

79. Audre Lorde, *A Burst of Light* (Ann Arbor: Firebrand Books, 1988), 60–61.

80. Ibid., 61.

81. Ibid., 127.

82. Jane Kenyon, *Otherwise: New and Selected Poems* (St. Paul: Graywolf, 1997), 214.

83. Havel, *Letters to Olga*, 9.

84. Ibid., 100–101.

85. Ibid., 10.

86. Ibid., 44.

87. Ibid., 48.

88. Ibid., 110, 112.

89. Michael Mallory, *Our Improbable Universe* (New York: Thunder's Mouth Press, 2004), 169.

90. Ibid., 10.

91. Dickinson, *Final Harvest*, 123.

92. William Sloane Coffin, *Credo* (Louisville: Westminster John Knox, 2004), 18.

93. Havel, *Letters to Olga*, 230–31.

94. Wilfred Cantwell Smith, *Faith and Belief* (Princeton: Princeton University Press, 1979), 20.

95. Sharon Daloz Parks, *Big Questions, Worthy Dreams: Mentoring Young Adults in Their Search for Meaning, Purpose, and Faith* (San Francisco: Jossey-Bass, 2000), 24.

96. Ibid., 7.

97. Doris Donnelly, "The Season of Hope," in *Weavings* 14, no. 6 (November/December, 1999).

98. Mark Doty, *Heaven's Coast: A Memoir* (New York: Harper Collins, 1996), 218–19.

99. Parks, *Big Questions, Worthy Dreams*, 19.

100. Lynch, *Images of Hope*, 245.

101. Quoted in Kingsolver, *Small Wonder*, 202.

102. Walter Brueggemann, *Hopeful Imagination: Prophetic Voices in Exile* (Minneapolis: Fortress Press, 1986), 95.

103. Ibid.

104. Williams, *The Open Space of Democracy*, 3.

105. Ibid., 10.

106. Michael Downey, "Gifts Constant Coming" in *Weavings* 14, no. 6 (November/December, 1999).

107. Groopman, *The Anatomy of Hope*, 179.

108. Mary Oliver, *Why I Wake Early: New Poems* (Boston: Beacon, 2004), 8.

109. Parks, *Big Questions, Worthy Dreams*, 19.

110. Griffin, *What Her Body Thought*, 37.

111. Thomas H. Maugh II, "Chronic Fatigue Is in the Genes, Study Finds," *Los Angeles Times*, April 21, 2006.

112. Thomas H. Maugh II, "Chronic Fatigue Linked to Genes," *Los Angeles Times*, in *Seattle Times*, April 21, 2006.

113. Kenyon, *Constance*, 25.

114. Wendell Berry, "The Peace of Wild Things," in *Poems to Live By in Uncertain Times*, ed. Joan Murray (Boston: Beacon, 2001), 43.

115. Kingsolver, *High Tide*, 16.

116. Patricia Hampl, untitled poem displayed at The Loft Literary Center, Minneapolis.

117. Eduardo Galeano, "Betrayal and Promise," *New Internationalist*, January 1999, 1.

118. Solnit, *Hope in the Dark*, 61.

119. Arthur Frank, *The Wounded Storyteller: Body, Illness, and Ethics* (Chicago: University of Chicago Press, 1997), 53.

120. Havel, *Letters to Olga*, 242.

121. Frankl, *Man's Search for Meaning*, 55.

122. Griffin, *What Her Body Thought*, 14.

123. See Diane Wolkstein and Samuel Noah Kramer, *Inanna, Queen of Heaven and Earth: Her Stories and Hymns from Sumer* (New York: Harper & Row, 1983).

124. Richard Cohen, *Blindsided: Lifting a Life above Illness: A Reluctant Memoir* (New York: Harper-Collins, 2004), 171.

125. Groopman, *The Anatomy of Hope*, 188.

126. Griffin, *What Her Body Thought*, 27.

127. Ibid., 14.

128. Dominique-Bauby, *The Diving Bell and the Butterfly*, 55.

129. Martel, *Life of Pi*, 204.

130. Doty, *Heaven's Coast*, 218–19.

131. Lynch, *Images of Hope*, 63.

132. Groopman, *The Anatomy of Hope*, 120.

133. Ibid.

134. Studs Turkel, *Hope Dies Last: Keeping the Faith in Difficult Times* (New York: New Press, 2003), 15.

135. Etty Hillesum, *An Interrupted Life* (New York: Holt, Rinehart and Winston, 1996), 152.

136. Desmond Tutu, *No Future Without Forgiveness* (New York: Doubleday, 1999), 35.

137. Ibid., 85.

138. Martel, *Life of Pi*, 169.

139. Mary Hembrow Snyder, ed., *Spiritual Questions for the Twenty-first Century: Essays in Honor of Joan D. Chittister* (Maryknoll, N.Y.: Orbis Books, 2001), 70.

140. Adrienne Rich, *Dark Fields of the Republic: Poems* (New York: W. W. Norton, 1995), 4.

141. William Stafford, *The Way It Is* (St. Paul: Graywolf, 1998), 139.

142. Malcolm Gladwell, *The Tipping Point: How Little Things Can Make a Big Difference* (New York: Little, Brown & Co., 2002), 258.

143. Solnit, *Hope in the Dark*, 4.

144. W. H. Auden, *The Prolific and the Devourer* (Hopewell, N.J.: Ecco, 1956), 98.

145. Charlayne Hunter-Gault, quoted in West, *Restoring Hope*, 65.

146. Ibid., 74.

147. Bourgeault, *Mystical Hope*, 72–73.

148. Parker Palmer, *Let Your Life Speak: Listening for the Voice of Vocation* (San Francisco: Jossey-Bass, 2000), 64.

149. Anne Lamott, *Traveling Mercies: Some Thoughts on Faith* (New York: Pantheon, 1999), 143.

150. Michael Downey, "Gift's Constant Coming," *Weavings* 14, no. 6 (November/December, 1999).

151. William Sloane Coffin, "Abounding in Hope," in *The Collected Sermons of William Sloane Coffin: The Riverside Years, Vol. 2* (Louisville: Westminster John Knox, 2008).

152. Hillesum, *An Interrupted Life*, 187.

153. Gerald May, *The Dark Night of the Soul: A Psychiatrist Explores the Connection between Darkness and Spiritual Growth* (New York: HarperCollins, 2005), 193–94.

154. Bourgeault, *Mystical Hope*, 79.

155. The Trocmé story has been chronicled in a film, *Weapons of the Spirit*, as well as in two books: *The Courage to Care*, by Carol Rittner and Sondra Myers (New York: NYU Press, 1989), and *Lest Innocent Blood Be Shed*, by Philip Hallie (New York: Harper Torch Books, 1985).

156. Etty Hillesum, *The Letters and Diaries of Etty Hillesum, 1941–1943*, ed. Klaas A. D. Smelik, trans. Arnold J. Pomerans (Grand Rapids: Eerdmans, 1986), 545.

157. W. H. Murray, *The Scottish Himalayan Expedition* (London: J. M. Dent and Sons, 1951), 6–7.

158. Marcia Prager, *The Path of Blessing: Experiencing the Energy and Abundance of the Divine* (Woodstock, Vt.: Jewish Lights, 2003), 13–14.

159. Emily Dickinson, quoted in Sewall, *The Life of Emily Dickinson*, 720.

160. Solnit, *Hope in the Dark*, 136.

161. Havel, *Disturbing the Peace*, 181.

162. Bourgeaut, *Mystical Hope*, 79.

163. Ibid., 87.

CPSIA information can be obtained
at www.ICGtesting.com
Printed in the USA
FFHW011352131219
56865283-62529FF